INFLATION AND PROFIT CONTROL

How to Account for Inflation in Business

INFLATION AND PROFIT CONTROL

How to Account for Inflation in Business

P. BAKKER

METHUEN
Toronto • London • Wellington

THE LAW BOOK COMPANY LIMITED
Sydney • Melbourne • Brisbane

Methuen
ISBN 0-458-91140-2

The Law Book Company Limited
ISBN 0-455-19323-1

Printed and Bound in Canada by
The Bryant Press Limited

1 2 3 4 5 6 7 4 9 8 7 6 5 4

CONTENTS

Foreword vii

Preface ix

1. Inflation and the Current Value Concept
1.1 What is inflation? 1
1.2 The effects of inflation on private enterprise 2
1.3 The effects of inflation on shareholders 3
1.4 The concept of profit 6
1.5 The concept of current costs 15
1.6 Valuation of assets 20
1.7 The effects of inflation on planning and on investment decisions 24
1.8 The effects of inflation on income taxes 27
1.9 Custodial versus managerial accounting 29

2. Accounting System in Trading Enterprises
2.1 Based on historical costs 35
2.2 Based on current values 36
2.3 Current values and fluctuating inventories 38
2.4 LIFO and fluctuating inventories 40
2.5 Current values and standard costs 41
2.6 Standard costs and accounting 43
2.7 Standard costs and fluctuating inventories 46

3. Accounting System in Trading Enterprises (Continued)
3.1 Monetary assets and current values 49
3.2 Difference between current values of assets and equity 51
3.3 Variations in current values and standard costs at year end closing 53
3.4 Inventories lower at year end 55
3.5 Inventories higher at year end 58
3.6 Obsolescence and current values 59
3.7 Frequency of value adjustments 61

4.   Comparative Summary of the Effects of the Different Concepts of Profit
4.1   Introduction   63
4.2   Financed by equity funds only   63
4.3   Financed by equity and other funds   65
4.4   Excess of monetary assets over liabilities   68
4.5   Comparative summary of profits under various concepts and conditions   70

5.   Fixed Assets and Current Values
5.1   Land   71
5.2   Interest as a cost item   71
5.3   Buildings, machinery and equipment   74
5.4   Cost per contribution unit and asset valuation   75
5.5   Valuation of fixed assets when price level changes   77
5.6   Replacement prices not available or not applicable   81

6.   Manufacturing Operations and Services Under the Current Value Concept
6.1   Advantages of standard costs in manufacturing   83
6.2   Price level changes in manufacturing   84
6.3   Calculation of price indices   84
6.4   Application of price indices in manufacturing   86
6.5   Enterprises with several manufacturing departments   94
6.6   Multi-division companies   96
6.7   Overhead costs and current values   99
6.8   Service industries and current values   101

7.   Integration of Management and Custodial Accounting in One Accounting System
7.1   Introduction   103
7.2   System designed primarily for management accounting   103
7.3   Integrated system of accounts   110
7.4   System of accounts for more than two purposes   118

8.   Special Cases
8.1   Technological price decreases   119
8.2   Companies with foreign assets and income   122
8.3   Differential costs and current values   123
8.4   Summary and conclusions   126

9.   Applications of Current Value Concepts
9.1   Review   129
9.2   N. V. Philips' Gloeilampenfabrieken   132
9.3   Progress in England   142

Index   145

FOREWORD

Proponents of current value accounting will welcome Mr. Bakker's contribution to accounting literature as it is indeed time that the mechanics of a method of current value accounting were set out in an organized text and the practicalities of such a method made available for general appraisal. Enough has already been written about the weaknesses of our traditional historical cost method of accounting that we should be prepared to consider current value accounting as an alternative.

To those unfamiliar with European methods of current value accounting this book introduces concepts which they should find interesting and very worthy of study. Those who have some familiarity with these methods will be further impressed with the author's sense of their logic and significance.

Many accountants have hesitated to consider seriously the use of current value accounting because of anticipated difficulties with its application. Such hesitancy should be dispelled by the methods outlined in this book. Mr. Bakker has set out in detail how an organization might design its accounts to produce meaningful current value financial statements. The resulting system of accounts will enable the organization to measure the effect of inflation on its financial position, and if proper management decisions are taken, to protect itself from inflationary trends.

The author does not suggest that the current value approach is the only acceptable method of accounting. He indicates that different groups of financial statement readers are interested in different financial statements and proposes that company management would be in a better position to gauge performance and make decisions if current value accounting were used for internal reporting purposes. If the accounts are designed as outlined in this book they will have a flexibility which will allow the presentation of financial statements on either a current value or historical cost basis or any variant of the two.

Mr Bakker is particularly qualified to address the subject of current values and inflation accounting, having spent thirty-five years in the accounting and finance departments of the Philips organization. That company is corporate testimony to a method of current value accounting that can be used to good advantage and is appropriate in the decision-making process. What may seem like a revolutionary method of accounting to North Americans has been in actual use by Philips for several decades. Mr. Bakker is well justified in pondering why more accountants have not yet acknowledged the merits of inflation accounting for profit control by adopting current value techniques.

I have known Bob Bakker for twenty-two years in close professional association. Throughout that time I have been very conscious both of the depth of his practical knowledge of the subject he has chosen for his book, and also of the extent of his intellectual mastery of the subject. It is therefore no surprise to me that he has produced a work of high quality that should both stimulate thought and have a thoroughly practical application.

November 1974
Robert B. Dale-Harris, F.C.A.

Robert B. Dale-Harris is a partner and member of the Executive Committee of Coopers & Lybrand, a past President of The Institute of Chartered Accountants of Ontario, a former member of the Committee on Accounting and Auditing Research of The Canadian Institute of Chartered Accountants and a former Chairman of the Canadian Tax Foundation.

PREFACE

Howard Ross' book[1] *Financial Statements: A Crusade for Current Values* challenged me to try and make a contribution to the problems of how to implement the current value concept in the accounting system or *how to account for inflation in business,* since I have had some 25 years experience in dealing with this aspect of accounting.

Numerous articles and a few books have been published lately criticizing the conventional accounting systems for their failure to cope with inflation and with changing price levels, as well as for their failure to provide management with meaningful information for performance control, decision-making and planning purposes. But as far as I know, no comprehensive accounting procedure has been published in the English language on *how*, on one hand, to account for the effects of inflation on assets, and on the other, on the equity and income of a business enterprise.

It is not the purpose of this book to discuss any of the publications on inflation or to explore the causes and cures of it. The sooner we accept the fact that inflation is going to stay with us whether we like it or not, the sooner we shall develop a philosophy of accounting which recognizes that the dollar is not a fixed, unchangeable *measure* for values, like the pound for weight and the yard for length.

Since no fixed measure for values has been found to replace the variable dollar, the accounting procedures must be adapted in such a way that the changing purchasing power of the dollar is properly taken into consideration if management is to be provided with reliable information to enable it to function efficiently and effectively.

The deadlock which presently exists has been brought about by the conventional accounting rules developed predominantly under the influence of tax laws and as such based on historical costs. These rules are erroneously referred to as "generally accepted accounting principles" when, in fact, they are not real principles, but rather a collection of common practices or conventions. In order to break the impasse a philosophy must be adopted in which accounting is a mirror of events valued at their current economic significance. This requires the "expurgation" of the present tax rules from business accounting, a switch from historical cost to current value accounting.

The purpose of this book is to show the reader, in broad terms, how to adapt the accounting system to current values, sometimes referred to as fair values or real values. Since a system without principles is inconceivable, the first chapter explains how the principles underlying current values should be the basis of accounting. The subsequent chapters deal with the techniques of recording, analyzing and presenting the business events on the basis of current values.

Most of this book is not new and a great deal of it is common practice in continental Europe, particularly in the Netherlands, where the principles of business economics serve as a foundation for accounting. Tax accounting in Europe is completely segregated from the other objectives of accounting. But also much in the English literature had a bearing on the contents of this book.

Without pretending to have all the answers to current value accounting I hope at least to "get the ball rolling" in an attempt to find a practical solution to the problem of how to account for inflation, and to revitalize accounting as a tool for management and profit control.

The assistance given in the final editing of this book by Franklin T. Hoare, President of The Carswell Company, is gratefully acknowledged.

P. Bakker

Chapter 1

INFLATION AND THE CURRENT VALUE CONCEPT

1.1   What is Inflation?

Inflation is a situation in which *prices rise* while the purchasing power of the dollar *diminishes*.

The prices of all economic goods, merchandise and services do not rise uniformly, as inflation is only one of the many factors that affect prices. Even in times of inflation, the prices of certain goods and services may decline due to an abundance of supply. This situation frequently occurs with agricultural products because of favourable weather conditions or technological breakthroughs in production. Also, the reverse is possible. In the absence of inflation the prices of certain goods and services rise due to counteracting forces, such as bad weather, war and strikes.

Inflationary situations differ for each individual and enterprise; for some the price increases may be higher than for others, or higher or lower than the average price level increases as indicated by the *Consumer Price Index* (cpi) or by the Gross National Expenditure (gne) *Implicit Price Index*. The first index is calculated monthly and the latter one quarterly.

The reason that inflation causes considerable difficulty is not so much a result of the phenomenon of inflation itself, but rather due to the fact that the dollar — as well as all other currencies — is supposed to be used as a neutral economic good against which all other economic goods can be exchanged. Simultaneously it is considered a yardstick by which to measure the value of economic goods in much the same way as a pound is used to measure weight or feet to measure distance. A misconception has developed, strengthened in times of stable price levels, that the dollar is a yardstick similar to those mentioned above. This misconception is unfortunate because the world has not yet been able to conceive a real and stable value-measure.

In the meantime, we have to accept the dollar as an imperfect value-measure, attempt to recognize its defects, do something to neutralize their effects and live with it as a normal phenomenon.

How to neutralize the effects of inflation in private enterprise, particularly in the area of management information for the decision-making process, is the subject of this book. However, before entering into a discussion of the actual accounting procedures involved, it is first necessary to highlight the effects of inflation on the enterprise and its interested parties — owners, shareholders, management, personnel, customers and suppliers of goods and services — the effects of inflation on profitability (earning power) and the effects of inflation on taxation. This will set the stage for underlining some principles of managerial accounting which will serve as a guide for implementing the "neutralization" process in accounting terms.

1.2   The Effects of Inflation on Private Enterprise

The effects of inflation on a business enterprise, in particular on the value of its assets and income, depend on its objectives. If the objective is to make a profit from a single "one-shot" affair, as for instance the construction of a building, the profit is simply the difference between the revenue and the expenditures; that is, between the cash received for the job and the cash spent on it. After distributing the profit and returning the equity, if any, to the enterpreneurs, the enterprise ceases to exist. In this case the profit is based on the historical cost concept. Since no assets are left there is no valuation problem.

However, if the objective of the business enterprise is to provide the interested parties with a *continuous income*, the situation becomes quite different. The income — in the form of dividends, salaries or wages — must be economically adequate to keep the "alliance" together, at least at a level in which the parties involved may be able to obtain remuneration in an alternative way; the shareholders by investing their equity in more profitable enterprises or in bonds, the managers and personnel in better-paying employment. The same applies, although to a lesser degree, to customers and to suppliers of goods and services. A business enterprise that is profitable establishes confidence with its suppliers, a requisite for obtaining credit. An enterprise that is able to live up to its obligations with respect to delivery times, quality and service attracts and maintains a dependable clientele.

In order to meet these requirements, the enterprise must conserve its income-producing facilities, or in other words, replace its resources as soon as they are consumed. Selling prices must be high enough to provide the enterprise with:

1. *A minimum income*, as defined in the third section of this chapter,

2. *Enough funds to replace the used resources* in order to safeguard the *continuity* of the enterprise. *This is an important principle, based on economic facts.* The principle of continuity will frequently turn out to be one of the cornerstones of the managerial accounting concept, in particular, with respect to the *income concept* and the *valuation of assets.*

Under this principle it becomes quite evident that the cost of the used resources is actually the cost to replace them, which in a trading enterprise is the *current market price,* or in the case of a manufacturing enterprise, the *current prices* of materials, labour, facilities and other elements of cost. Obviously, it is *not* the *historical price,* the price paid for them in the past.

For example, if the historical purchase price of a product was $100, the current market price is now $110, and the selling price is $115. The profit is $5, not $15, since $110 is required to restore the inventories involved to their original volume, a necessity for an *uninterrupted continuation* of the business enterprise. Thus, the *value of an asset* is not what was paid for it in the past, but the *current price*, which is identical to the *replacement price*, or as it is more commonly called, the *replacement cost*.

However, if the enterprise is *discontinued*, as already explained in a one-time transaction, the replacement price is irrelevent as a basis for valuation or income determination, because replacement is not required.

The replacement price could also be irrelevant in a going concern when *replacement is not possible* for technical reasons, or not desirable for economical reasons, such as obsolete facilities or products. Here replacement cost is either not available or irrelevant. The current value of the assets in this case is obviously what can be *realized*; that is, the net proceeds after deducting the costs involved in the realization.

For example, the selling price of a certain model of men's winter coat is reduced towards the end of the season from $200 to $120, in order to dispose of the remaining inventory of this model. The original purchase price was $100, whereas additional coats of the same model could be purchased from the supplier for $110. The costs of selling are 30% of sales. Accordingly, the *realizable* value or *net proceeds* amounts to $84 ($120 less 30%). Since this is lower than the replacement cost, the inventory should be valued on the basis of net proceeds, $84 for each coat.

The valuation principle consists of *replacement cost and net proceeds, whichever is lower,* and is a variant to the conventional accounting rule of *cost (historical cost) and market, whichever is lower.* The application of the principle "replacement cost and net proceeds, whichever is lower," to other assets such as physical plant which will not be replaced by identical assets, but in due course by other more productive and more efficient facilities, is less easy than for inventory. In Section 1.6 we return to this point.

Another effect of inflation or rising price levels is that the book values of the assets of a business enterprise gradually become meaningless and thus irrelevant for presenting a fair picture of the *financial position* of the enterprise. The fair value of a going concern is of great significance for the present and potential future shareholders, for financiers, for suppliers and for management. To meet with their requirements, the assets on the balance sheet must be valued on the basis of current values that are relevant to the environment in which the enterprise operates.

1.3 The Effects of Inflation on Shareholders

An investor will generally buy shares in a business enterprise for two reasons: dividends and capital gains. His purchase is based on the expectation that the dividends and capital gains combined will, on average, provide a yield that is at least equal to alternative investment opportunities; this is the minimum income required. Because of the risk factor, a higher yield can be expected from shares than from bonds. For the sake of simplicity, the average shareholder is considered here since the personal income tax aspect for the individual shareholder may vary considerably and, therefore, lead to different conclusions with respect to his investment choices.

It may be assumed that when all profits of a company are paid out, the market price of its shares will approach the intrinsic value (current value) of the shares if the yield is equal to that in an alternative investment opportunity, disregarding a difference in risk factors, income and capital gain tax considerations as well as temporary market price fluctuations. If the yield is higher, the market price will accordingly rise and exceed the intrinsic value of the shares. If the yield is lower than that in an alternative investment opportunity, the market price will be lower than the intrinsic value.

If part of the profit is retained in the business, resulting in an increase in the current value of the shares, the combined yield of dividends and capital gains will remain the same. Accordingly, the market price of the shares, abstracted from other influences, will remain the same as well. However, the profits retained by the company increase the equity, and assuming that the profitability (earning power as a percentage of equity) remains the same, the higher equity will lead to proportionately higher profits. On the basis of the previous pay-out ratio, this situation will lead to higher dividends and in turn to a higher market price.

Now, what is the effect of inflation on the position of the shareholder? In order to remain interested in the company in which he buys shares, he will expect to be compensated for the loss of purchasing power caused by inflation, either by higher dividends and/or by higher capital gains from higher stock market prices. Inflation causes the shareholder to suffer a loss:

1. On his original investment, and

2. On his original income.

An example may illustrate the effects of inflation better than a long exposé:

Inflation rate — 4% per year
Profit per share — $3.00
Dividend per share — $3.00
Current value per share — $50.00
Stock market price — $50.00
Profitability — 6%
Yield desired by shareholder — 6%

From this example we can deduce that there will be a loss on the original investment of $2.00 (4% of $50.00) and a loss on the original income of $0.12 (4% of $3.00). In order to remain in the same financial position, the nominal income should rise by $2.12, either in the form of a higher dividend or in an increased market value of the shares.

The company's profitability on the original equity of $50.00 in this example should increase from 6% to 10.24%. The 10.24% consists of:

1. 6% original profit

2. 4% to offset the inflation loss on the original investment

3. 4% of 6% (0.24%) to offset the inflation loss on the dividend.

With continuous inflation the dividend will also have to rise continuously. In the above-mentioned example is will rise successively to $3.12, $3.24, $3.37, $3.51 and so on, to offset a 4% inflation. To maintain the current value of the shareholders' equity and its earning power and to provide for continuously rising dividends, the 4% mentioned under Point 2 cannot be paid out to the shareholders, but must be added to the equity. In the first year this will amount to $2.00, the second year $2.08 (4% on $52.00), the third year $2.16 (4% on $54.08) and so on. Under the assumed conditions the market price in this example will rise in accordance with the current value of the shares and in this way compensate the shareholders for the inflation losses on the original investment.

The above illustration of the effects of inflation on shareholders in a public company is a very simplistic one; it merely serves to draw the attention of the reader to the fact that the company must increase its profits on a historical cost basis from $3.00 to $5.12 per share after tax, in order to conserve its earning power. This means that the pre-tax earnings, assuming a corporate income tax rate of 40%, must increase from $5.00 to $8.53 per share. In Section 1.8, the effects of inflation on corporate income taxes is further analyzed.

Returning to the original problem, the effects of inflation on the shareholder's position becomes more complicated if a part of the profit is retained by the company to finance a normal growth. The tables shown below illustrate what happens to the dividend and the current value of the shares if, in the above example, 60% of the profit is paid out and 40% is retained. Table 1 shows the pattern without inflation and Table 2 with 4% per year continuous inflation, all figures per share.

Table 1 *

Year	Profit	Dividend	Retained	Current value at		Combined yield †
				Beginning of year	Year end	
1	$3.00	$1.80	$1.20	$50.00	$51.20	6%
2	3.07	1.84	1.23	51.20	52.43	6
3	3.15	1.89	1.26	52.43	53.69	6
4	3.22	1.93	1.29	53.69	54.98	6

*Professor Dr. L. Traas, in an article in *De Accountant* (a monthly publication of the Netherlands Institute of Accountants) of September 21, 1972, uses a similar type of table to illustrate the effects of inflation on shareholders.
†In % of current value at beginning of the year.

Table 2

Year	Profit	Dividend	Retained	Current value at		Combined yield †
				Beginning of year	Year end	
1	$5.12	$1.87	$3.25	$50.00	$53.25	10.24%
2	5.45	1.99	3.46	53.25	56.71	10.24
3	5.81	2.12	3.69	56.71	60.40	10.24
4	6.18	2.26	3.92	60.40	64.32	10.24

†In % of current value at beginning of the year.

If the profitability of the company is different from the desired yield, which may be considered the rule rather than the exception, it will be reflected in the stock market prices of the shares. A higher profitability will result in a market price exceeding the current value, whereas a lower profitability will show up in a lower market price, disregarding other factors that may affect the market quotations.

Inflation has a similar effect on the shareholders of private companies with one exception. If a shareholder of a public company is not satisfied with the yield on his shares in the form of dividends, capital gains, rights and such, he can sell his shares, although probably at a loss, and seek other more profitable investment opportunities. This is difficult and in many cases impossible for shareholders in private companies without taking a large loss.

1.4   The Concept of Profit

Basic Principle

In Section 1.2 the *profit of a transaction* was defined as the difference between the selling price and the current value of goods sold. This provokes the question: "What is the nature of the difference between the current value and the historical price paid for the goods involved?" On the basis of the historical cost concept, this difference, assuming that the current value is higher that the original purchase price, is a part of the total *nominal* profit.

On the basis of the current value concept the latter part of this "profit" constitutes a part of the funds necessary to replace the goods sold, as illustrated in Section 1.2, provided it is the intention to continue the business. Accordingly, this part of the "profit" is not available for distribution unless the business is discontinued, in which event the continuity, which constitutes the basis for setting selling prices and profit control, is broken. From an historical or nominalistic concept of profit *these unrealized profits* are sometimes called "holding gains," and as such are not available for distribution in a going concern.

Nominal Profit

The total nominalistic profit of a period or the difference between the revenue from sales and the cost of sales based on historical cost during that period breaks down into the following two elements:

1. *Operating results or transaction results*, based on current values and thus reflecting the real performance of the operation

2. *Holding gains* brought about by the fact that the used resources were purchased at lower prices than those at which they were replaced.

This viewpoint may be further illustrated by a simple example:

The opening balance sheet of a trading enterprise shows:

1. Inventory — 10,000 pieces at $10 each	$100,000
2. Shareholders' equity	$100,000
During the year:	
10,000 pieces were purchased for	$105,000
10,000 pieces were sold for	$110,000
of which the current costs (at the time of sale)	
amounted to	$105,000

All transactions were on a cash basis and no expenses were involved. The current purchase price of this product at year end is $11 per unit.

The balance sheet at year end based on *historical costs* would appear as follows:

BALANCE SHEET

Inventory:		Equity	$100,000
10,000 at $10.50	$105,000	Operating profit	10,000
Cash	5,000		
	$110,000		$110,000

But with the assets valued at *current prices*:

BALANCE SHEET

Inventory:		Equity	$100,000
10,000 at $11.00	$110,000	Holding gains	10,000
Cash	5,000	Operating profit	5,000
	$115,000		$115,000

From these two balance sheets it is evident that:

1. The distribution of the $10,000 profit, based on historical cost, would *break up the continuity* of the enterprise, since it would compel the enterprise to liquidate part of the inventory in order to raise enough cash for the profit payout. In actual practice, this problem is generally solved either by paying out only part of the profit, by raising new equity funds or by borrowing.

2. Only the operating profit of $5,000 is *available for distribution*, since the holding gains or "revaluation surplus" of $10,000 is tied up in the inventory which, as assumed in this example, is required to safeguard the continuity of the enterprise.

It is not always as easy as illustrated in this example to break down the total nominal profit into holding gains and operating profit, as will be shown in subsequent chapters. *For managerial purposes it is imperative that attempts be made in this direction* in order to be able to provide insight for both management and shareholders into the actual performance of the business enterprise. Only the operating results are relevant to ascertain the real profitability of the shareholders' equity; as such the operating results constitute a reliable basis for forward planning and budgeting as well. But when these results are combined or mixed with the holding gains, the outcome is useless for responsible management decisions. In this regard I wholly agree with Ross'[2] quotation of the principle expounded by Keynes that "it is better to be vaguely right than precisely wrong," applied in this case to the segregation of the holding gains.

Holding Gains Concept

At this point one might consider the treatment of the holding gains that result from the revaluation of the physical assets (principally fixed assets and inventories). In this regard, two viewpoints are held — the Holding Gains Concept and the Equity Concept. In the former concept, the holding gains are considered as part of the equity, in which case the name might be changed to "revaluation surplus." The advantage of this concept lies in the simplicity of the procedure. After the current value of the assets has been determined at year end the difference between the book value and the current value of the assets is transferred to a "holding gains" account. The disadvantage is that the calculation of the holding gains is based on the actual assets on hand at year end. This method does not take into consideration the effects of temporary lower or higher assets than the enterprise normally would have at year end, nor does it take into consideration the losses caused by inflation when a substantial part of the equity is tied up in *nominal* (monetary) assets, such as accounts receivable and cash. An example may illustrate this problem:

> Assume that in the example provided earlier in this section the actual purchases amount to 6,000 items, instead of 10,000, at a total cost of $63,000. The other assumptions remain unchanged.

The inventory account would now appear as follows:

INVENTORY ACCOUNT

Jan. 1 Balance:			Dec. 31 Cost of sales:	
10,000 at $10.00	$100,000		10,000 at current value of	$105,000
Dec. 31 Purchases:			Dec. 31 Balance:	
6,000 at total cost of	63,000		6,000 at $11.00	66,000
Dec. 31 Holding gains	8,000			
	$171,000			$171,000

The balance sheet at year end:

BALANCE SHEET

Inventory:			Equity	$100,000
6,000 at $11.00	$ 66,000		Holding gains	8,000
Cash	47,000		Operating profit	5,000
	$113,000			$113,000

Analysing the differences between this balance sheet and the earlier balance sheet with an inventory of 10,000 items, it appears that:

1. The additional $42,000 cash results from 4,000 fewer items in inventory, of which the current value at the time of sale was $42,000. The average current purchase price during the year was $10.50 per unit each.

2. Assuming the company wants to restore the inventory to the same level as at the beginning of the year, the additional 4,000 items, if purchased at the year end at the then current price of $11.00 each, would cost $44,000, or $2,000 more than the available cash of $42,000 into which part of the inventory was converted during the year.

This leads to the conclusion that, in the event the continuity of the enterprise demands a normal inventory level of 10,000 pieces, a loss of $2,000 must be taken in order to restore the holding gains to $10,000. This reduces the *distributable profit* to $3,000 and leaves enough cash, $44,000, to replenish the inventory. If the inventory was reduced temporarily in anticipation of lower purchase prices at the time that replacement was imminent, then the $2,000 is a *speculation result* and should be shown as such in the financial reports.

Losses on Monetary Assets

It is also evident from this example that, in times of inflation, losses are sustained on monetary assets in so far as these are not offset by monetary liabilities, such as loans and trade accounts payable. These losses increase when physical assets are temporarily converted into monetary assets.

A serious case of this phenomenon is the amortization of the capital funds invested in fixed assets, as a result of which physical assets are gradually converted into monetary assets. If no provisions are made for the losses sustained on these monetary assets, the company will find itself eventually in a position where it does not have sufficient cash to replace the fixed assets. In this case it would seem that the amortization over the past years had been inadequate, for which reason some speak of a "depreciation gap"[3] or "under-depreciation gap" (more correctly called an "amortization gap" or "under-amortization gap"). In actual fact the so-called under-depreciation is caused by the diminishing purchasing power of the monetary assets into which the funds freed by amortization have been invested. Accordingly, this depreciation gap does not appear when the amortized funds are invested in other physical assets, or financed by loans for which the repayment coincides with the amortization of the fixed assets. In Chapter 5, "Fixed Assets and Current Values," Section 5.5 elaborates further on this point.

From the above, it would appear that in addition to the holding gains on the actual assets on hand, an amount should be set aside to offset the diminishing purchasing power of monetary assets (less liabilities) to the extent that these eventually will be re-used to replace those physical assets which have been temporarily converted into monetary assets. It is evident that a segregation of the monetary assets into two parts may turn out to be difficult or at least arbitrary. One part is reserved for the eventual replacement of physical assets and a balance remains.

Equity Concept

The concept of *holding gains* or *unrealized nominal profits* recognizes the assets of an enterprise as the *source of income* which under the commitment of continuity has to be preserved. The other viewpoint is that the *shareholders' equity* is the source of income, the purchasing power of which has to be conserved. The two concepts lead to different answers. Applied to the previous example, and assuming that the equity must be revalued by the same percentage as the assets, say 10%, the balance sheet would appear as follows:

BALANCE SHEET

Inventory	$ 66,000	Equity:	
Cash	47,000	Original	$100,000
		Revaluation	10,000
Revaluation loss	2,000	Current value	$110,000
		Operating profit	5,000
	$115,000		$115,000

This approach appears to be the simpler of the two, in that no separate calculation has to be made for the loss of purchasing power of the monetary assets, regardless of the origin of the large amount of cash on hand.

As long as the financing of the enterprise is exclusively or predominantly with equity funds, the results of the two concepts do not vary much. However, with a different capitalization for example, with 50% equity funds and 50% borrowed funds the results vary considerably, as shown by the two balance sheets below. For simplification, the interest on the borrowed funds is disregarded in this example.

Under the holding gains concept the balance sheet would read:

BALANCE SHEET

Inventory	$ 66,000	Equity	$ 50,000
Cash	47,000	Creditors	50,000
		Holding gains	8,000
		Operating profit	5,000
	$113,000		$113,000

As observed previously, the holding gains may have to be raised by $2,000 to offset the loss of purchasing power of that part of the available cash that arose from the temporary reduction in inventory. This, in turn, reduced the profit available for distribution to $3,000. Under the equity concept the balance sheet would appear as follows:

BALANCE SHEET

Inventory	$ 66,000	Equity:	
Cash	47,000	Original	$ 50,000
		Revaluation	5,000
		Current value	$ 55,000
		Creditors	50,000
		Revaluation surplus	3,000
		Operating profit	5,000
	$113,000		$113,000

It appears that under the equity concept, $5,000 of the holding gains have been used to revalue the shareholders' equity, leaving a favourable revaluation balance of $3,000, but the $3,000 cannot be considered a distributable profit under the continuity principle. To safeguard the continuity, $5,000 should be set aside. This results in a loss of $2,000 and reduces the distributable profit, as before, to $3,000. The $5,000 to be set aside is calculated as follows:

Revaluation of the inventory (see the inventory account on page 9 by	$8,000
Loss of purchasing power of the $42,000 cash emanating from the reduced inventory (see the calculation on page 10)	2,000
	$10,000
Less: revaluation of the equity by	$5,000
Balance	$5,000

From these examples it appears that neither the holding gains concept nor the equity concept automatically provides, under all circumstances, the right answer to the question of which part of the nominal profit and which part of the operating profit are available for distribution. When the enterprise is financed exclusively or predominantly with equity funds, the correct answer is found automatically as described previously in this section.

The best compromise seems to be to follow a course in which:

1. The revaluation of the physical assets is credited to a "revaluation surplus account".

2. This account is charged for the revaluation of the shareholders' equity.

3. The revaluation surplus account is credited with a provision to offset the loss of purchasing power of those cash reserves which are latently committed for replacement of fixed assets and inventories.

It is evident that, aside from the simplistic examples in this section, the estimate of the provision mentioned in Point 3 is bound to be global. However, as long as one understands the principles underlying the current value concept, a reasonably correct answer can always be found.

Two Equity Revaluation Concepts

With the revaluation of the equity one can take the view that the current value of the equity should be based on the current value of the assets, or that the current value of the equity should be based on the general purchasing power of the dollar as indicated by the Consumer Price Index or the GNE Implicit Price Index. In other words, the equity should be adjusted to reflect the *specific rate of inflation* (or price level changes) to which the particular enterprise involved is subjected, or alternatively the equity should be adjusted to reflect the *general rate of inflation*.

Adjusting the equity on the basis of the *specific price index* would come close to the "holding gains method," since the holding gains reflect the price level changes of the assets. Adjusting the equity on the basis of the *general rate of inflation* recognizes the *origin of the equity*, namely the shareholders. We have seen in the previous section that the shareholder is interested in the conservation of his equity to provide him with a continuously inflation-proof income which he expects to be at least as high as any he can obtain in alternative investment opportunities. In this regard, he is not interested in the specific rate of inflation his company is subjected to.

When the general rate of inflation is adopted for revaluation of the shareholders' equity, a revaluation variance will arise if the specific rate of inflation applied to the revaluation of the assets is different. In this concept an unfavourable variance should be considered a loss and deducted from the operating profit to prevent an erosion of the equity, whereas a favourable variance should be set aside as a reserve since this may be tied up in the assets and, as such, cannot be distributed as a profit without depleting the funds necessary to continue the operations. It is even conceivable that this reserve should be increased by a provision to offset the loss of purchasing power of the monetary assets committed to replenish the used resources to their normal level, as illustrated on pages 11 and 12. The following chapters, which are based on this concept, will enter into greater detail.

The total (nominalistic) profit of a period under the "holding gains" concept consists at this stage of:

1. Operating results.

2. Holding gains, representing unrealized differences between historical costs and current values of remaining capital assets, plus a provision for the loss of purchasing power of the monetary assets committed to the continuation of the enterprise

and under the "equity" concept, based on the general rate of inflation of:

1. Operating results

2. Revaluation surplus or deficit, due to
    2.1 Different price indices for assets and equity
    2.2 Provision for the loss of purchasing power of the monetary assets committed to the continuation of the enterprise.

Breakdown of Operating Results

In both concepts there is no difference in the calculation of the operating results which, in an accounting system based on standard costs, may be broken down into the following components:

1. Transaction results; revenues less standard costs adjusted to current value.

2. Residual income; the difference between the imputed interest charge on the investment in the operating assets and the interest paid on loans, if any (This is further discussed in Section 1.5).

3. Performance variances; differences between actual performance and standard or budgeted performance.

4. Volume variances, due to a higher or lower load than the normal capacity load level, used as a basis for setting standard costs.

5. Purchase price variances.

6. Lifetime variances on capital assets.

7. Speculative results.

8. Other operating results.

A difference may arise between the accumulated holding gains under the one concept as compared to the cumulative equity adjustments and revaluation surplus under the other concept. This may happen as a result of a drastic change in the assets of the enterprise due, for example, to a technological breakthrough in the manufacturing process. In this case the holding gains concept, which is based on the assets as the source of income, may show results different from the equity method, which is based on the equity as the source of income without, however, losing sight of the facilities and other resources which are the means to create the income. Chapter 8, "Special Cases," will enter in greater detail on this aspect of current value accounting.

Profit Determination and Profit Appropriation

Not relevant to the objective of this book, but still worthwhile mentioning is the distinction between *profit determination*, which is one of the most important objectives of managerial accounting, and *profit appropriation*. Profit determination is a purely *retrospective* affair, whereas the appropriation may be influenced by *plans for the future*, such as an imminent expansion in which case it may be decided to reduced the profit payout or substitute a stock dividend for a cash dividend.

1.5   The Concept of Current Costs

A clear concept of profit is important, but to make this concept work in practice, it is necessary to have a clear concept of the components of profit as well; namely, revenues and costs.

Determining profit in a "one-shot" deal is very simple. Total cash revenue less total expenditures is profit, although, if equity capital is involved, the entrepreneur might want to reduce the nominal profit by a certain amount to offset the loss of his equity capital's purchasing power during the time it took to make the deal.

In principle, the same procedure of profit determination could be followed by a going concern. If one could wait until the very end when the business enterprise is wound up, the same formula as in the "one-shot" deal could be applied. However, this is not normally possible. Management must know how well the enterprise is doing; it has to establish prices and to plan for the future, while the shareholders expect a financial report and dividends from time to time.

Accrual Method of Accounting

The solution to the necessity of reporting on a periodic basis is found by the *accrual method* of accounting. This is a procedure in which the flow of values through the enterprise is substituted for the *cash flow*. Profit is now defined as the favourable difference between *revenues and costs*. The billings to customers are substituted for the cash receipts to determine the revenue, whereas costs are the value of the resources used in the business process. The determination of the latter is the most difficult as it involves the measurement of the quantities of used resources, such as material, contributions of facilities to the process, the time involved, etc., as well as the valuation of these quantities.

Objectives of Cost

Costs — or rather cost prices for products and services — are both used retrospectively to determine the operating profit of a period and to enable management to make decisions and to plan for the future.

Cost prices are used to establish selling prices if the enterprise is the "price leader" in the industry and for profit control if the enterprise is a "price follower." Cost prices of products and services are also used for "make-or-buy" decisions as well as for planning and budgeting.

Different Costs for Different Purposes

Cost prices may be different for different purposes. For example, expansion plans should be based preferably on *full costs (integral costs)*, or at least on the additional costs (including the probable increase in general administrative costs) brought about by the expansion. As long as these costs plus a desired margin are lower than the additional revenue expected to be generated by the expansion, the expansion is justified.

Under normal conditions, full cost will also be used by the price leader in the industry as the basis for establishing his selling prices, whereas the price followers, in order to obtain the most profitable load for their existing facilities, may want to compare the attainable prices with their variable costs. In other cases, for example in export markets or private brand markets, to obtain additional orders for under-loaded facilities, the selling prices may be based on the *additional costs (differential costs)* these orders bring about. Any excess of revenue over the additional costs incurred constitutes a contribution to fixed overheads and profit which, in the short run, may have a significant effect on financial results.

In other words, a business enterprise cannot apply one uniform cost formula to all occasions that may arise in decision-making and in forward planning. When the enterprise uses a standard cost system, which has great merit for performance control and inventory control, management must realize that the standard costs may need to be adjusted to fit the occasion when used for decision-making, such as establishing a pricing policy and for forward planning.

There are various types of standard cost systems.[4] The system based on *normal conditions* is an excellent application of the *replacement cost* concept, which as explained before represents the current value in all those cases in which replacement is possible and intended. To be acceptable and useful the replacement cost concept must be based on three principles which also form the basis of the normal standard cost concept, namely, the principles of:

1. *Continuity*, or "going concern" concept,

2. *Normality*,

3. *Fairness*.

The first principle has been mentioned earlier as a basis for valuation, requiring the application of replacement costs rather than actual or historical costs if replacement is possible and intended. The second principle refers to normal operating conditions, to normal quantities of materials, services and time, to a normal level of performance and efficiency and to a normal activity level, all with reference to the particular enterprise involved. This means that different enterprises will have different costs, due to variations in size, location and other operating factors. The normality principle applied to costing excludes everything that is not rational, such as avoidable wastes of time and materials, avoidable shrinkage due to poor workmanship, avoidable breakdown of facilities, and poor maintenance. The third principle is less a principle than an attitude of the staff involved in setting standards of performance, as the basis for costing, and in the valuation of the quantities involved. Costing is generally an arbitrary activity, in that one may be more inclined to the conservative or to the optimistic view of the quantities and the values involved. To stay repeatedly on one side may have a lopsided effect. Fairness demands an average course. Fairness also implies that costing procedures must be immune to undue influences by the persons who either use the cost information in their decisions or planning, or who are being judged on their performance on the basis of the cost information.

Although the purpose of this book is not to offer a comprehensive treatise on the art of cost accounting, there is still one important aspect that is hardly ever mentioned in the English literature — costs, by their nature, have three "dimensions:"

1. The *quantities* required for replacement or reproduction; standard quantities of the resources involved.

2. The *value*; current value of the resources.

3. The *time*; during which the capital funds invested in the means of production (fixed assets, inventories, accounts receivable, etc.) are normally engaged in the replacement or reproduction process.

Interest Charge in Costs

The third "dimension," which involves the inclusion of an *imputed interest charge* in the cost, is generally considered controversial. However, in Section 1.2, it was established that adequate income is necessary to ensure the continuity of an enterprise. This income should be at least as high as the suppliers of the capital funds could have obtained in alternative investment opportunities. Hence, the imputed interest charge, as far as equity capital is involved, is an "opportunity" cost. The engagement of capital funds in a business process is as indispensable as the use of facilities, materials, labour and services. For that reason, it must be concluded that an interest charge for the use of capital funds is a *genuine element of cost*, regardless of whether interest and dividends are paid or not. This is a basic principle, and as with other principles in this regard, is *normative* in that it is *fundamental* to the *economic concept of cost* of a going concern. These principles would not apply to a company in the process of liquidation.

Rate of Interest

The question may be raised now as to what a normal rate of interest would be. The answer is the *minimum rate* obtainable in an alternative opportunity; in other words, the current rate, which is the rate the company would have to pay to replace existing capital funds (equity and borrowed funds). With respect to the cost of equity funds, the corporate income taxes should be taken into account. Companies that include an interest charge in the cost generally calculate an average of the actual rate paid on borrowed funds, if any, and of a normal dividend on the shareholders' equity. This is based on opportunity cost plus the corporate income taxes payable on a normal dividend.

Example:
    Assume a capitalization as follows:

Shareholders' equity at current value of	$1,000,000
Opportunity yield 6%	
Income taxes 40%	
Loans at a current rate of 8%	$1,000,000

From this follows:

Opportunity costs of	$ 60,000
Income taxes 40/60 x $60,000	40,000
Interest on loans	80,000
Total current cost of capital funds	$ 180,000

$$\text{Working out at a rate of } \frac{180,000}{2,000,000} \times 100 = 9\% \text{ per year}$$

The profit which a company makes over and above $60,000 after taxes, in the above example, is sometimes called *residual income*.

Interest Charges on Specific Projects

Thus, in this example, the standard costs will include an imputed interest charge of 9% per year on the current value of the assets. However, if a separate loan is obtained to finance a specific project and the repayment of the loan coincides with the amortization of the capital funds invested in the project, then it is obvious that the imputed interest charge to be included in the cost of operating this project should be equal to the actual interest rate payable on the separate loan.

Price Fluctuations

Once a standard cost system has been installed, a problem arises as soon as the current values of the components of the standard costs begin to *deviate* to such an extent that the calculation both for income determination and for decision-making, in particular sales pricing and profit control, becomes unreliable. To change the standard costs each time the current prices fluctuate more than a tolerable amount is generally not efficient. For the purpose of performance control, which relies mainly on quantities and less on values, the tolerance is probably 10% as far as values are concerned. However, for profit control and sales pricing the tolerance may be as low as 1% or 2%.

A far better solution than changing the standard costs involves the application of *price indices* to the standard costs, in which the given standard cost level is 100. These price indices can be reviewed and brought up to date quarterly and, when price fluctuations are severe, at monthly or even shorter intervals. A price index system not only saves a considerable amount of effort but is also a much faster method of keeping management continuously informed with respect to the current price levels. In Sections 2.6 and 6.3 examples are given for calculating price indices and applying them in the accounting process.

For planning and budgeting purposes it is not recommended to attempt a forecast of the future price levels. Apart from the fact that these forecasts must be highly arbitrary, an additional speculative element is also introduced into the plans and the budgets.

It is easier and more realistic to base plans, budgets and standard costs on the current values existing at the time that these plans, budgets and standards are prepared and to adjust them when and if the need arises, either entirely or by the use of price indices. In Section 1.7 we return to this subject in more detail.

1.6 Valuation of Assets

A proper valuation of the assets of an enterprise is of great importance in showing a fair picture of the financial position of the enterprise to present and future shareholders, management, creditors and other interested parties. A balance sheet based on historical costs not only distorts the real financial position of a company in that it is a summary of dollars of varying values, but it may even be misleading.

A fair picture can only be achieved by converting the historical dollars of varying values to the common denominator of the current value of the dollar as at the date of the financial statements.

Current Values are Relevant Values

The assets should be valued at current values or prices which are relevant to the situation of the company and to its assets at a given date. It is pertinent to know whether we are dealing with a going concern or a company in liquidation. The value of the assets of the latter type of company is obviously that which the owners can obtain from selling off the assets, less expenses to be incurred in the liquidation process. The assets of a going concern, however, have a value for the future as a means of earning income. As such their value is either determined by the cost of replacing them or, if this is not determinable for technical or technological reasons, or is not intended for economic reasons (such as obsolete products), by what they will yield in selling them off or in using them up. In all cases we are dealing here with relevant or current values, either replacement cost or net proceeds.

The principles underlying the current value concept are, as all principles, very simple and clear, but their proper application is occasionally difficult and sometimes seems even impossible. However, this is no reason not to try it. In the end, one must realize that valuation is not an exact science, but is the *best possible approximation* of the true value.

When the replacement of assets is considered to be *rational* in a going concern, they can be valued at:

1. The current market price; this applies to all purchased and current (not obsolete) inventories of materials and products.

2. The current cost of replacement or reproduction; this applies to manufactured goods and work in process:
   2.1 At full costs for inventories of goods forming a part of the normal business activies,
   2.2 At differential costs for inventories of goods specially made for additional business in different markets; for example, export markets and private brands markets.

3. The current market price for fixed assets less an allowance for depreciation caused by wear and tear and for economic obsolescence based on the estimated lifetime of the assets involved.

Character of Fixed Assets

There is a principal difference between materials and fixed assets. Materials can be used only once in a business process, whereas fixed assets can be used repeatedly until they become technically worn out or economically obsolete. From the viewpoint of valuation, fixed assets can be considered as a *series of contributions* or service units to the business process which, for technical reasons, have to be purchased in one lot but can be used gradually until their contributions are exhausted. For that reason, the current value may be considered as the *present value of the future contributions*, which on the day a fixed asset is purchased is supposed to be equal to the purchase price. In accordance with this viewpoint the capital funds devoted to fixed assets should be amortized on the basis of the *annuity method*. Chapter 5, "Fixed Assets and Current Values," elaborates upon this method.

Land Values

The current value of land should be based on the market value. Changes in land values come slowly under normal economic conditions. If no price is readily available, an appraisal once every 5 or 10 years may be adequate.

Net Proceeds as a Basis for Valuation

Assets which *cannot be replaced* by identical assets for technical reasons or will not be replaced for economical reasons should be valued on the basis of their *net proceeds*, since this is their *economic value* to the enterprise. The first category refers to assets which are no longer available, having been replaced by different, probably more modern, assets. The second category refers to assets which could be replaced, but have become obsolete because more productive or more efficient assets have become available since the purchase of the original assets. The second category also refers to inventories of materials and products that have become obsolete due to design changes, age, fashion, over-purchasing and the like.

As previously mentioned, current value in these cases is the net proceeds which will be realized from the sale of the assets. The proceeds can be either *direct* or *indirect*, as follows:

1. *Direct proceeds* apply to those assets having a market price. These encompass products which are becoming unfashionable or obsolete and will be sold at reduced prices, including used equipment such as automobiles and scrap. The current value of these assets is the expected gross proceeds less anticipated selling expenses.

2. *Indirect proceeds* apply to those assets which are not intended to be sold as such, but which will be used as long as they are expected to make an *economic contribution* to the enterprise. Their value is the *present value* of all their future contributions. There are two different groups of assets that come under this principle:

    2.1 Individual assets which generate independent income such as a building, a truck, or a ship,

    2.2 Complementary assets connected with other assets, as with various machines and equipment, each one of which is a link in an integrated manufacturing process.

It should not be too difficult to calculate the present value of separate assets. Generally it is possible to calculate or estimate the value of one economic contribution, such as a square foot of floor space of a building per year or a ton-mile of freight for transportation equipment, and further to estimate the probable life span that is still left in the assets involved. With the aid of compound interest tables and a desired interest percentage, the present value can then be determined. Chapter 5, "Fixed Assets and Current Values," gives an example of this method of asset valuation. If assets of this kind have a market price as well, which is conceivable for buildings and transportation equipment, then of course the lower of the two valuations, present value or market price, should apply. On the other hand, if the market price appears to be higher than the present value to the enterprise, it is evident that the asset should be sold and replaced for economical reasons.

A difficult problem concerns the valuation of the assets referred to in Point 2.2 above. The only solution takes into account the valuation of the entire group as one asset, making certain allowances for the degree of wear and tear of the individual items, since this may vary considerably.

It appears that the *valuation of all fixed assets*, except those that are to be sold soon or to be scrapped, is based on the same principle; namely, that the *current value is the present value of the future contributions* of the assets to the operations. Another important conclusion that can be drawn from the current value concept is that the interest factor is an integral aspect of it. This can be noted from a viewpoint of asset valuation and income determination as well as for planning purposes and for investment decisions (See Section 1.7).

Price Level Restatements by Index Method

In actual practice the valuation of current (not obsolete) fixed assets is generally based on the original purchase price adjusted for price level changes, if any, by using a price index that is applicable to the situation in which the company happens to be, less depreciation based on the estimated lifetime. The correct depreciation or, rather, amortization method is, of course, the *annuity method* which gives due recognition to the current costs; that is, interest costs of the capital funds devoted to these assets. It is seldom possible to obtain a market price for specific fixed assets. For that reason the use of an appropriate price index to adjust the book values of the assets to current values saves considerable time and effort. More time can be saved by a classification of the assets by production or cost centre, and by lifetime group; this considerably facilitates the allocation of the monthly or annual amortization and interest charges.

Balance Sheet and Income Statement Products of One Process

It becomes more and more evident that the valuation of assets is closely related to the determination of income. Thus, the balance sheet and the income statement should be the products of *one* accounting procedure. In this respect the concept of management accounting differs fundamentally from the concept of custodial accounting.

Obsolescence and Valuation

In Section 1.4, which dealt with the concept of profit, it was stated that the adjustments to the current value of the assets caused by inflation or by price level changes should be considered as "holding gains" or, in a different manner, should be applied against the adjustment of the shareholder's equity.

Not every revaluation of an asset is due to inflation. Another reason is obsolescence, both inventories and fixed assets, which has nothing to do with inflation or price level changes. A certain degree of obsolescence is a regular and unavoidable cost of doing business and as such should be segregated from the effects of inflation. With respect to materials and products, the best way to account for the cost of obsolescence is to set up a provision account which is credited with a standard percentage of the cost of sales for products and of the cost of materials used in manufacturing, and charged with the amounts of the assets written off as obsolete. A balance in the "provision for obsolescence" expressing a better or worse performance than the standard should be treated as a "performance variance" in the income account. With fixed assets it happens regularly that one asset has a shorter than expected lifetime, due to technical or economical reasons, whereas another asset has a longer than expected lifetime. If amortization and interest charges are based on the estimated lifetimes of the assets, but the charges are continued only for the actual lifetimes, variances will occur due to differences between estimated and actual lifetimes. The favourable and unfavourable variances emanating from this should be respectively credited and charged to a *fixed assets lifetime variance account.* A favourable balance that is increasing during a couple of years points to an underestimation of the average lifetimes, whereas an unfavourable balance would point to the opposite. Repeated deficits in the account should be taken as a loss and the estimated lifetimes should be adjusted accordingly.

Segregating the effects of inflation from the effects of obsolescence of the fixed assets may turn out to be rather arbitrary. However, a fair approximation will suffice for managerial purposes.

1.7   The Effects of Inflation on Planning and on Investment Decisions

Long range planning, as well as budgeting for a shorter period, is by no means made easier by changing price levels and inflation. It adds one more uncertainty about the future of the enterprise. What should be done about this? Ignore it and cross the bridge when one comes to it by adapting the plans and raising selling prices on the basis of up-to-date current cost information? Or attempt to estimate future price levels and subsequently prepare long range plans and on those bases?

The latter course is not recommended because as mentioned in Section 1.5, it introduces a highly *speculative* factor into the calculations. The first course is safer; plans, budgets, standards and other calculations with respect to the future activities should be based on the price levels relevant at the time the plans and calculations are prepared, with subsequent revisions at certain intervals.

Strategic Planning

However, there may be certain recognizable trends in the course of changing price levels that may make it useful or even compelling, to do some "strategic" planning in exploring alternative courses under varying circumstances that may occur and from which certain definite conclusions can be drawn at the outset concerning the direction that the enterprise should take. Strategic planning is also necessary in choosing a location for future growth, in choosing products and in make-or-buy decisions under conceivably varying conditions.

With respect to changing price levels, it may appear that the personnel costs, including the cost of fringe benefits, are rising faster than the costs of other factors. This should be taken into consideration in investment decisions by putting a greater emphasis on mechanization and automation than one otherwise would do. An example may illustrate this:

A machine is approaching the point that it must be replaced. The company has the choice to replace the machine by a similar machine (Machine I) or by a different more automated type (Machine II). The costs involved are as follows:

	Machine I	*Machine II*
Cost of purchase and installation	$100,000	$400,000
Operating costs per year	$100,000	$ 25,000
Estimated lifetime	5 years	5 years

It is estimated that the average price increase in the cost of the machines will be 5% per year; the increase in operating costs consisting mainly of personnel costs is expected to be 8% per year. The cost of capital funds is assumed to be 10% per year.

The advantage of Machine II involves a saving on the operating costs of $75,000 per year. Ignoring future price levels, the present value of the savings over a period of 5 years at an interest rate of 10% would be $284,300. This is less than the additional purchase cost of $300,000 for Machine II, leading to the conclusion that the purchase of Machine I is more economical. However, if a cost increase of 8% per year is expected and included in the calculation, the present value of the savings is $328,700 leading to an opposite conclusion!

Difficulties in Later Verification of Planning Savings

Inflation can be misleading, as shown in the annual figures concerning the costs of Machine II, which on one hand seem to confirm the accuracy of the conclusion that the purchase of Machine II is more economical than Machine I, but not on the other hand. This depends on whether the conventional method of accounting, based on historical costs, or the current value method of accounting is applied. In the two tables below, all figures are based on current values in accordance with the previously assumed yearly price increase of 5% for machines and 8% for the operating costs, except for the annuities in the first table, which are shown in the *conventional* method. The amortization of the capital funds invested in the machines is based on the 5-year 10% annuity table.

Table 3: Based on the Conventional Accounting Method

	Year					Total
	1	2	3	4	5	
Machine I						
Annuity	$ 26,380	$ 26,380	$ 26,380	$ 26,380	$ 26,380	$131,900
Other costs	100,000	108,000	116,640	125,970	136,050	586,660
Total I	$126,380	$134,380	$143,020	$152,350	$162,430	$718,560
Machine II						
Annuity	$105,520	$105,520	$105,520	$105,520	$105,520	$527,600
Other costs	25,000	27,000	29,160	31,490	34,010	146,660
Total II	$130,520	$132,520	$134,680	$137,010	$139,530	$674,260
Savings I – II	−$4,140	+$1,860	+$8,340	+$15,340	+$22,900	+$44,300

The present value of the balance of the annual savings and losses at the beginning of the first year, based on an interest rate of 10% per year, amounts to $28,700. It is assumed that the annual savings are realized at year end; actually they would of course arise gradually during the year and not at year end, in which case the present value of the savings in this example would be somewhat higher.

However, it is imperative the author advocates that, for the pricing of sales, profit control and the calculation of transaction results, all costs should be calculated at current price levels. This applies to not only the (out of pocket) operating costs but also the capital costs (amortization and interest charges) of the machines. If, in accordance with this principle the books of account reflect current values as well, the following picture would emanate from these accounts:

Table 4: Based on the Current Value Method of Accounting

	Year					Total
	1	2	3	4	5	
Machine I						
Annuity	$ 26,380	$ 27,700	$ 29,084	$ 30,539	$ 32,065	$145,768
Other costs	100,000	108,000	116,640	125,970	136,050	586,660
Total I	$126,380	$135,700	$145,724	$156,509	$168,115	$732,428
Machine II						
Annuity	$105,520	$110,800	$116,336	$122,152	$128,260	$583,068
Other costs	25,000	27,000	29,160	31,490	34,010	146,660
Total II	$130,520	$137,800	$145,496	$153,642	$162,270	$729,728
Savings I – II	−$4,140	−$2,100	+$228	+$2,867	+$5,845	+$2,700

According to this table, in which the annuity (amortization and imputed interest charges) is increased by 5% each year in order to reflect the current price level of the machines, the accumulated savings would add up to only $2,700.

But when the annual holding gains or revaluation adjustments plus the interest on these gains compounded at 10% per year during the 5 year lifetime of the machine are taken into account, the decision to buy Machine II appears to be justified. The annual increases of 5% in book value of Machine II, less those of Machine I, amount to $34,610 and the interest to $6,990, making a total of $41,600:

	Machine II	*Machine I*	*Difference*
Annual adjustments	$46,148	$11,538	$34,610
Interest at 10%	9,320	2,330	6,990
Total	$55,468	$13,868	$41,600

The annual adjustments to the book value are transferred to "holding gains" or "revaluation surplus," and the interest on these gains is transferred to the imputed interest account. The difference of $41,600 plus the savings of $2,700 based on current costs shown in Table 4, a total of $44,300, coincides with the *nominal* savings, based on *historical* annuity costs, shown in Table 3 above.

In the accounts the following collective journal entry of the current costs of Machine II would be made (See Table 4):

Machine costs	$729,728	
Amortization of machinery and equipment		$400,000
Holding gains		46,148
Interest imputed		
1. On funds originally devoted to investment in machines		127,600
2. On holding gains invested in machines		9,320
Cash		146,660
(With regard to other operating costs)		

This example proves that checking whether or not an earlier investment decision was correct should not be based on the current accounting figures only, but that the holding gains and interest on these gains must also be taken into account.

1.8   The Effects of Inflation on Income Taxes

The Income Tax Act of Canada as well as tax legislation in most other countries does not recognize the effects of inflation on the profitability of companies nor on the income of investors, be they shareholders or lenders.

The actual tax rate for a company in a period of inflation is higher than the nominal tax rate because the calculation of taxable income is based on *historical* costs. The concession to shareholders of Canadian companies to deduct 50% of the capital gains on shares is an *inadequate* compensation for the loss of purchasing power. The interest which the owner of bonds receives, although in part compensation for the loss of purchasing power of the bonds, is fully taxable.

The effects of inflation on the company's income can best be demonstrated by an example:

Operating profit before income taxes is $5 per share. The tax rate is 40% of income based on historical cost. Current value of the equity is $50 per share entirely invested in physical assets.

The increase in the effective rate appears in the table below, in which three different cases are compared:

	No Inflation	4% Inflation	10% Inflation
Per share:			
1. Operating profit	$ 5.00	$ 5.00	$ 5.00
2. Holding gains	–	2.00	5.00
3. Taxable income	$ 5.00	$ 7.00	$10.00
4. Taxes at 40%	2.00	2.80	4.00
5. Net profit (1–4)	$ 3.00	$ 2.20	$ 1.00
6. Effective tax rate as a % of 1			

Corporate Income Taxes Accelerate Inflation

The company in this example could try to pass the extra tax burden as well as the increased capital cost (See Section 1.3) on to the customers in order to retain the *original rate of return*. This would show the following picture:

	No Inflation	4% Inflation	10% Inflation
Per share:			
1. Net profit	$ 3.00	$ 3.00	$ 3.00
2. Loss of purchasing power on:			
Net profit	–	.12	.30
Equity (of $50.00)	–	2.00	5.00
	$ 3.00	$ 5.12	$ 8.30
3. Tax at 40%	2.00	3.41	5.53
4. Taxable income	$ 5.00	$ 8.53	$13.83
5. Extra tax burden	–	$ 1.41	$ 3.53
6. Extra capital cost	–	0.12	0.30
7. Extra cost to customers if the company wants to retain its original profitability	–	$ 1.53	$ 3.83

It is quite evident from this example that if the company wants to retain its original rate of return (6% of the current value of the equity in this example) the extra tax burden will have to be recovered through higher prices to customers. In this way the Canadian Income Tax Act accelerates the inflationary forces by increasing the tax burden out of proportion to the rate of inflation. If the company cannot recover the added tax burden, the rate of return may diminish to a point where additional equity capital for expansion cannot be raised and where employment opportunities suffer.

Income Tax Laws Should be Inflation-Proof

It would be fairer and more realistic to increase the tax by the same percentage as the rate of inflation, from $2 to $2.08 and $2.20 instead of to $3.41 and $5.53. This would remove the spiraling effect that the present tax law now brings about.

The issue of bonds rather than shares may not be the answer to off-setting the effects of inflation as a result of high interest rates. These rates necessarily include a premium to offset the loss of purchasing power as well as the extra income taxes on this premium.

It would be fairer to companies, shareholders and bondholders, if corporate taxes were made "inflation-proof," as the Government of Canada now proposes to do for personal income tax. Corporate income taxes could just as easily be made inflation-proof by allowing companies to reduce the gross nominal income based on historical cost by an amount equal to the loss of purchasing power of the shareholders' equity, as indicated by the increase in the Consumer Price Index. As with the proposal to make personal income taxes "inflation-proof," a similar change in corporate income taxes would bring to an end the present conflict of interest situation, in which the government benefits from inflation, and the taxpayers, both customers who have to pay higher prices and the companies whose profitability is endangered, suffer from it. Obviously, companies are now forced to raise prices to keep up their level of profitability and to maintain the interest of their shareholders.

It should be realized that unless corporate tax laws are changed to allow for inflation, the only beneficiary of inflation will still be the tax collector. A good example in this respect is set by other countries such as France, Sweden and Brazil who have long since enacted legislation that provides tax relief from effects of inflation to a considerable degree.

1.9 Custodial Versus Managerial Accounting

Custodial Accounting Concept

It may be said that at present financial statements of most enterprises are the products of what is commonly called *custodial accounting*. This concept is basically concerned with the preparation of reports and data for groups or persons other than management. It includes the preparation and presentation of reports to shareholders as well as to creditors and tax authorities.

This concept of accounting is based mainly on what is allowed by the existing tax laws; as such both valuation of assets and determination of profit is based on *historical* costs. Of course, no one can object to a fair attempt at reducing taxes by taking full advantage not only of what the tax laws expressly allow, such as the accelerated amortization of fixed assets as a means to stimulate the economy in certain circumstances, or by taking advantage of loopholes in the tax laws. This has become an exciting "sport" between the parties involved, the taxpayers and the tax collectors, in which the taxpayers are supported by tax consultants, in particular the public accountants, so enthusiastically and devotedly that the other objective of the art of accounting, that is, performing as a tool of management, has long since suffered from "malnutrition."

However, it is not the objective of this book to criticize the prevailing accounting concepts further in their failure to support management. This has been done adequately in numerous articles and books, many of which have come to the conclusion that custodial accounting is inferior in concept to management accounting.

Management Accounting

In management accounting the area of interest concerns the way in which the accounting concept can be updated to perform its most important function — that of providing management with reliable information for performance control, decision-making and planning. This is the concept of *management accounting or managerial accounting.* A comprehensive concept of management accounting includes the limited objectives of custodial accounting as well. This point is explained in greater detail in Chapter 7, "Integration of Management and Custodial Accounting in One Accounting System."

The objective of managerial accounting is to record, to analyse and to project economic facts in accordance with accounting principles based on sound business economics. Part of the information of this accounting concept is *retrospective* in nature, involving, in part, the determination of the periodic results and the financial position of the enterprise, and in part is *prospective* in nature, involving cost prices and other information for business planning and budgeting. A fundamental difference between custodial accounting and managerial accounting is that the first is strictly retrospective, whereas the latter is both retrospective and prospective.

The information to be generated by a comprehensive management accounting system can be summarized in more detail as follows:

Retrospective Information

1. Period results on a per year, per month, etc. basis, broken down into:
    1.1 Operating results, based on current value,
    1.2 Revaluation results, or holding gains or losses.

2. The amount of income that can be paid out without trespassing on the source of income.

3. A breakdown of operating results:
   3.1 By responsibility or operating area,
   3.2 By product group or similar classification,
   3.3 Into actual performance against standards and budgets, classified into:
       3.31 Performance or efficiency variances,
       3.32 Volume variances,
       3.33 Price variances,
       3.34 Speculative results.

4. Analysis of the operating results and causes in variations from standards and budgets.

5. Preparation of periodic statements of the financial position and of the operating results for interested parties — management at the various levels, shareholders, creditors, tax authorities and other governmental agencies.

Prospective Information

1. Detailed cost information based on current values for:
   1.1 Sales pricing and profit control,
   1.2 Make-or-buy decisions,
   1.3 Investment decisions,
   1.4 Performance standards and budgets.

2. Further information for the preparation of long range plans, budgets and performance standards.

This is a long and incomplete list. However, it should be realized that the extent of some details, such as the elaborate analysis of the operating results, depends to a large extent on the size, the diversity and the dispersion of the enterprise. In very small enterprises a great deal of the information required for managerial control is obtained by direct supervision and communication which in larger enterprises must be replaced by other means such as standards and budgets, and other types of organization such as profit centres.

Principles Underlying Current Value Concept

In the previous sections of this chapter, we touched upon a few principles underlying the concept of current value which serve as a guide for the application of the current value concept and for the development of the necessary accounting conventions and rules. While the principles are of a fundamental nature in that they apply to all enterprises, the accounting rules may vary to suit the specific type of enterprise. Probably the word "convention" expresses more clearly the nature of the rules, which is to make the application of the accounting principles *convenient*. Some examples of conventions are that debit is on the left side of the ledger and credit on the right side, the so-called accrual method of accounting which converts the cash flow into a flow of values, and formulas for cost allocation and cost proration. Principles say *why*, whereas conventions or rules say *how* to account for economic facts. To repeat and elaborate upon some of the discussion in Section 1.5 of this chapter, the current value concept of accounting, or managerial accounting, is based on the following principles:

1.   Continuity

We are dealing with a going concern, not with an enterprise in the process of liquidation. Accordingly, the value of an asset is equal to either:

    1.1 The cost of replacing it, if replacement is possible and intended, or to

    1.2 The net proceeds, direct or indirect, if replacement is not possible or not intended.

2.   Normality

Values or costs should be based on normal operating conditions, normal performance and efficiency, and economical lot sizes in purchasing and manufacturing. This concept excludes economically avoidable waste in the use of resources. In retrospect waste is a loss and a better-than-normal performance is a profit. Both should be excluded from the normal (standard) value or cost of an asset, such as a product, or for sales pricing or business planning. Although there are different definitions or interpretations of "normal," for the purposes of a first attempt at introducing the current value concept it is sufficient to say that the normal is a rational average that excludes economically avoidable waste.

3.   Fairness

Fairness applies to both principles and conventions. Almost every valuation is arbitrary and subject to an element of uncertainty. It is not at all difficult to come up with two or three different cost prices for the same product due to the application of different conventions in cost allocations, each one of which can be reasoned as correct. The accountant must have the strength of character and the wisdom to express a fair and equitable judgment of the correct value. However, one must realize that *accuracy* in the sense of an accurate value is a *myth*. Also, that accuracy, to the extent that accuracy of the information is feasible, is of lesser importance than *reliability, relevancy* and *timeliness* of information. In this respect, the accountant must be a valuator rather than a chronicler of historical facts. An important aspect of fairness in the computation and presentation of information is that of consistency. When a change is made a good reason for the change should be clearly stated.

Three Current Value Concepts

In the application of the current value concept, there are, as mentioned in Section 1.4 of this chapter, three choices in showing the effects of inflation on the financial position of the enterprise:

1. The holding gains concept.

2. The equity concept, based on the *specific* inflation to which an enterprise is subjected.

3. The equity concept based on *general* inflation as expressed by a purchasing power index, such as the Consumer Price Index or the GNE Implicit Price Index.

The following chapters explain step-by-step the implementation of the current value concept in the accounting system. They are based on the equity concept in Point 3 above, while occasionally showing the difference in outcome under one of the other two concepts. This does not mean that the other two concepts should be disregarded. In this regard more research may be required to find the ultimate truth.

Chapters 2 and 3 deal with the implementation of current values in trading enterprises; Chapter 4 summarizes in some detailed schedules the profit under different concepts and under varying conditions; Chapter 5 discusses the valuation of fixed assets; and Chapter 6 explains in some detail the application of current values in manufacturing enterprises. Chapter 7 explains how custodial accounting, based on historical costs, and managerial accounting based on current values, can be integrated into one accounting system. Chapter 8 deals with special cases, which for reasons of simplicity, were not included in the preceding chapters. Chapter 9 highlights some actual applications of the current value concept. The accounting procedure in all chapters is designed to provide both the balance sheet and the income account as two products of *one* accounting procedure.

Notes

1. Published by Sir Isaac Pitman (Canada) Ltd. in 1969.
2. Howard Ross, *Financial Statements: A Crusade for Current Values.* (Pitman, 1969), page 33.
3. Fraser Robertson used this term in the Toronto *Globe and Mail* on March 9, 1971 in an article "Financial Reporting and Real Money Values".
4. R. J. Dickey, *Cost Accountant's Handbook.* New York; The Ronald Press Company, 1960, Chapter 15, "Setting Standard Costs".

Chapter 2

ACCOUNTING SYSTEM IN TRADING ENTERPRISES

2.1 Based on Historical Costs

A simple example may be used to illustrate the difference between the conventional accounting system based on *historical costs* and the accounting system based on *current values*:

January 1, 1973:

Inventory on hand 10,000 pieces at $10 each	$100,000
Shareholders' equity	$100,000

Transactions during 1973:

Purchases, evenly spread over the year, at gradually rising prices (from $10 to $11), 10,000 pieces at an average purchase price of $10.50 each, total cost	$105,000
Sales, 10,000 pieces, total proceeds	$110,000

All transactions are on a cash basis and no expenses are taken into account.

It is assumed in this example that the inventory turns over once per year, as a result of which the goods on hand at the beginning of the year are sold during the year, and the goods purchased during the year constitute the inventory on hand at the end of the year. Under the pure historical cost rule of first-in, first-out, or FIFO for short, the cost of goods sold during the year in this example amounts to $100,000 and the historical cost of the closing inventory amounts to $105,000. After posting all entries, the inventory account, under the historical cost rule, appears as follows:

INVENTORY ACCOUNT 1973

Jan. 1 Balance:		Dec. 31 Cost of sales:	
10,000 at $10.00	$100,000	10,000 at $10.00	$100,000
Dec. 31 Purchases:		Dec. 31 Balance:	
10,000 at $10.50	105,000	10,000 at $10.50	105,000
	$205,000		$205,000

The profit and loss account will appear as follows:

PROFIT AND LOSS ACCOUNT 1973

Cost of sales	$100,000	Sales	$110,000
Operating profit	10,000		
	$110,000		$110,000

The balance sheet at year end will appear:

BALANCE SHEET AS AT DECEMBER 31, 1973

Inventory	$105,000	Equity	$100,000
Cash	5,000	Operating profit	10,000
	$110,000		$110,000

The profit under the application of the historical cost rule appears here as $10,000.

2.2   Based on Current Values

Under the current value principle, as explained theoretically in Chapter 1, "Inflation and the Current Value Concept," profit for a certain period is the excess of the *current value* of the assets less liabilities over the current value of the *shareholders' equity*. The application of this principle implies that used resources must be costed at their current value, in our example at the cost to *replace* the goods sold. The real cost of goods is not what was paid for them in the past, but the current value which the enterprise is surrendering at the time of sale in order to produce revenue.

To illustrate the application of this principle, both in its effect on the balance sheet and on the income (profit and loss) account, refer back to the example of the previous section. Assume further that the current value of the shareholders' equity as at December 31, 1973, is 10% higher than a year earlier and that the purchase price of the goods at year end is also 10% higher, or $11 each. The opening balance sheet as at January 1, 1973, is the same as in Section 2.1. After all the entries for 1973 have been posted, the inventory account under the current value concept appears as follows:

INVENTORY ACCOUNT 1973

Jan. 1 Balance: 10,000 at $10.00	$100,000	Dec. 31 Cost of sales: 10,000 at $10.50	$105,000
Dec. 31 Purchases: 10,000 at $10.50	105,000	Dec. 31 Balance: 10,000 at $11.00	110,000
Dec. 31 Revaluation adjustment	10,000		
	$215,000		$215,000

The average price to replace the goods sold during 1973 amounted to $10.50, in total $105,000. The purchase price or the current price at year end is $11 per unit. Accordingly, the current value of the inventory at year end amounts to $110,000. This requires an adjustment to the inventory account of $1.00 per unit, or a total of $10,000. The shareholders' equity account must be adjusted as well by 10% of the opening balance of $100,000, or $10,000.

Since we assumed in this phase of our explanations that the effect of inflation was exactly the same on goods as on the equity, and further that the entire equity was invested in goods, it is no accident that both adjustments are for the same amount and offset each other. In more complicated cases, which will be illustrated in the following pages, it is recommended to use a "revaluation adjustment account," to which all adjustments may be transferred.

The profit and loss statement for 1973 under the application of the current value principle would now appear as follows:

PROFIT AND LOSS ACCOUNT 1973

Cost of sales, at purchase prices current when sales are made during 1973	$105,000	Sales	$110,000
Operating profit	5,000		
	$110,000		$110,000

The balance sheet at year end will appear:

BALANCE SHEET AS AT DECEMBER 31, 1973

Inventory, at current prices	$110,000	Equity:	
		Original	$100,000
Cash	5,000	Adjustment	10,000
		Current value	$110,000
		Operating profit	5,000
	$115,000		$115,000

Effect on Profit Available for Distribution

The most striking feature that occurs when comparing this balance sheet with the one in Section 2.1 is that the amount of profit in periods of inflation and under the conditions assumed in our example, as determined under the current value concept, is lower than it would appear to be under the historical cost rule. Another fact pointed up here is that, under the historical cost concept, the amount of cash generated during 1973 is not sufficient to pay out the entire profit. Apparently a part of the profit, $5,000 in our example, was needed to finance the higher inventory costs.

Under the application of the current value concept the *real situation of the enterprise* is shown; namely, the amount of profit is available in cash. If this entire profit were to be paid out, the continuity of the enterprise would not be jeopardized. To pay out the entire profit based on historical cost would force the enterprise either to borrow money or to sell off part of the inventory, which would erode the shareholders' equity and endanger the continuity of the enterprise.

LIFO-Rule

Under the application of the inventory rule of last-in first-out, or LIFO for short, the amount of profit would be exactly the same as under the current value principle. This is true only when goods are immediately replaced at the time of sale, or in other words, when purchases and sales are ideally synchronized and therefore the inventory level does not fluctuate. The effect of fluctuating inventories on the profit and loss account will be illustrated in the following two sections, under the current value concept and under the LIFO-rule respectively.

Application of the LIFO-rule does not entail a revaluation of the assets or of the shareholders' equity; consequently the balance sheet does not reflect the economic facts. In times of rising prices the value of the inventory and the equity would both be understated.

2.3 Current Values and Fluctuating Inventories

In our examples of the previous sections assume that the inventory level fluctuates due to delayed purchases, as in the following illustration:

Quarter	Quantity Purchased	Purchase Price Each	Total Amount Paid
1	—	—	—
2	1,000	$10.40	$ 10,400
3	4,000	10.60	42,400
4	5,000	10.80	54,000
Totals	10,000		$106,800

Sales are spread evenly over the year. After all entries have been posted, the inventory account appears as follows:

INVENTORY ACCOUNT 1973

Jan. 1 Balance:		Dec. 31 Cost of sales, at
10,000 at $10.00	$100,000	replacement costs:
		10,000 at $10.50 $105,000
Dec. 31 Purchases:		
10,000 at total cost of	106,800	Dec. 31 Balance:
		10,000 at $11.00 110,000
Dec. 31 Revaluation adjustment	10,000	
		Dec. 31 Loss 1,800
	$216,800	$216,800

The $10,000 charge to the inventory account represents the revaluation of the inventory from $10 (the price at which the inventory was valued on January 1, 1973) to $11 per unit; accordingly for 10,000 pieces a charge of $10,000. After entering the closing inventory at the current price of $110,000 the inventory account shows a debit balance of $1,800, representing a loss due to delayed replacement of the sold merchandise. This may be verified by the following table:

| Quarter | Quantities | | | Cost Prices | | | |
	Sold	Bought	Difference	Actual	Annual Average	Difference	Loss *
1	2,500	—	−2,500	$10.20	$10.50	−$0.30	$ 750
2	2,500	1,000	−1,500	10.40	10.50	− 0.10	150
3	2,500	4,000	+1,500	10.60	10.50	+ 0.10	150
4	2,500	5,000	+2,500	10.80	10.50	+ 0.30	750
Totals	10,000	10,000	—				$1,800

*Difference in quantities x difference in cost price.

To make a calculation like the one above for a variety of products takes time and becomes rather complicated when the inventory levels at the end of the year are higher or lower than at the beginning of the year. However, this problem can easily be solved by the use of standard costs, a concept discussed later in this chapter. The purpose of the above simplified example is to show the reader how the principle underlying the current value concept is applied, as well as to show how this principle differs from the historical cost rule and the LIFO-rule. The latter is frequently recommended as a substitute for the current value concept, but it is not.

The profit and loss account in this section shows a trading profit of $5,000, the difference between sales of $110,000 and the replacement cost of $105,000, and a loss of $1,800 due to delayed purchases. If the fluctuation in inventories is caused by speculative buying, the results should be shown as "speculation results." Results of this nature should be segregated from the regular trading results to promote a better insight into the causes of the operating results.

The balance sheet at year end now appears as follows:

BALANCE SHEET AS AT DECEMBER 31, 1973

Inventory, at current prices	$110,000	Equity:		
Cash	3,200	Original		$100,000
		Adjustment		10,000
		Current value		$110,000
		Trading profit	$5,000	
		Less:		
		Loss due to inventory fluctuation	1,800	
		Operating profit		3,200
	$113,200			$113,200

2.4 LIFO and Fluctuating Inventories

Under the LIFO-rule the cost of sales in the previous section would have been calculated as follows:

Quarter	Quantity Sold	Last Actual Purchase Price	Cost of Sales
1	2,500	$10.00	$ 25,000
2	1,500	10.00	15,000
	1,000	10.40	10,400
3	2,500	10.60	26,500
4	2,500	10.80	27,000
Totals	10,000		$103,900

The inventory account under the LIFO-rule would appear as follows:

INVENTORY ACCOUNT 1973

Jan. 1 Balance:		Dec. 31 Cost of sales:		
10,000 at $10.00	$100,000	10,000 at total cost of	$103,900	
Dec. 31 Purchases:		Dec. 31 Balance:		
10,000 at total cost of:	106,800	10,000 at total cost of:*	102,900	
	$206,800		$206,800	

*The closing balance consists of	
6,000 pieces at $10 each	$ 60,000
1,500 pieces at $10.60 each	15,900
2,500 pieces at $10.80 each	27,000
10,000 pieces	$102,900

The closing balance represents neither the historical cost of the stock on hand nor the current market value. It is a mixture of both and really of little use to anyone interested in the financial position of the particular business, which is evident from the following balance sheet, based on the LIFO-rule:

BALANCE SHEET AS AT DECEMBER 31, 1973

Inventory	$102,900	Equity	$100,000
Cash	3,200	Operating profit*	6,100
	$106,100		$106,100

*Balance of $110,000 sales and $103,900 cost of sales.

Objections to LIFO-rule

The average business enterprise usually carries an inventory that consists of a few fast-moving items and many slow-moving items. The application of the LIFO-rule would, in periods of rising prices, overstate the operating profit considerably.

In Summary, the LIFO-rule

1. Provides a balance sheet that does not reflect the economic facts.

2. Distorts the income statement.

3. Does not provide an analysis of the income into trading results and other (speculative, in our example) results.

Due to these shortcomings, the LIFO-rule should be rejected as a basis for accounting. The LIFO-rule cannot be qualified as a *principle* of accounting, for a principle must be logical and, in accounting, provide a reliable balance sheet simultaneously with a reliable income account. The current value principle provides both.

2.5 Current Values and Standard Costs

Advantages of Standard Costs

In enterprises with a great variety of articles such as finished products, work in process, sub-assemblies, parts, raw materials and repair and maintenance materials, the use of standard costs and standard prices has a number of advantages, the most important of which are:

1. Financial inventory control is greatly facilitated.

2. Costing of sales and materials used in manufacturing is simpler.

3. A useful yardstick is provided to measure operating performance, especially in manufacturing.

In times of increasing or decreasing price levels for salaries, wages, materials, services and other costs and expenses, management must at all times be kept informed of the *current price level* in order to make the correct decisions with respect to sales policies, pricing sales, profit control, making or buying, replacement of facilities and planning.

Standard Costs Not Always Up-to-date

The standard costs and standard cost prices can never be kept quite up-to-date. In enterprises of average or larger size, the standard costs are generally reviewed once a year. Because a revision takes time, it is not unusual that the review of these prices is started some months before the beginning of the period to which they will apply. For instance, in a company that manufactures a variety of products, the accountant may have to review the standard costs of the purchased materials and parts in October in order to be able to have all standard costs completely updated by the 1st of January. Before the accountant begins with the revision of the standard costs, he must make a decision with respect to the price level upon which the standard costs will be based. Should this be the average price level of the past 3, 6, 9 or 12 months, or the price level on the very day that he begins with the revision? Or should he incorporate the price level that he, in consultation with management and on the basis of an expert forecast of the economy of the country and of the particular industry to which the company belongs, expects to prevail during the period to which the revised standard costs will apply?

The easiest solution is to base the standard costs on the price level of the very day on which the revision is begun. The price level of a past period is probably less suitable, perhaps due to technological changes in the manufacturing processes or in the product designs. In any event, price levels of a past period are no longer current. On the other hand an estimate of the price level that will prevail in the period under consideration may turn out to have been incorrect due to its speculative nature. The best solution is to base the standard costs on the current price level.

Co-ordination of Standard Costs with the Current Price Level

As long as the current level of prices, salaries, wages and services does not deviate more than a fraction, say one-half to one percent from the basis upon which the standard costs were set, there does not seem to be much of a problem in using the standard costs for managerial decisions. However, when the price level of one or more of the components of the standard costs goes up or down to such a degree that the standard costs are no longer considered to be reliable enough for decision-making, there are two ways of coping with this problem.

One method is to revise those standard costs which have deviated from the current price level by more than the acceptable tolerance. The other solution is to keep the standard costs unchanged, but to use *price indices* with the standard costs as 100. The first approach is recommended in those enterprises which deal in one or only a few commodities or services, where a frequent updating can be done quickly and without a great deal of work. The second approach is generally more efficient for companies with a variety of goods. For many manufacturing companies with a long list of materials, the use of price indices is the only solution to keep management informed at all times about the current price and cost levels.

Price Index System

The calculation of price indices for trading enterprises can be kept quite simple. The calculation of price or cost indices for manufacturing concerns requires more work and will be explained in some detail in Chapter 6, "Manufacturing Operations and Services under the Current Value Concept."

For the preparation of price indices in trading enterprises, the merchandise should be classified into groups which are homogeneous with respect to fluctuations in the purchase prices. The condition of homogeneity of a group is met when the component parts of each product are proportionally similar, for example, rubber shoes and canvas shoes in a footwear business. The price index of a group can be established in two different ways:

1. As a weighted average of all members of the group, or

2. On the basis of a prototype.

The first method requires considerably more work than the second method, and must be followed in case the group is not so homogeneous that a prototype, that is to say one product (or material) which may be considered representative of the entire group, can be used as a basis for the price index. If the first method is used, a considerable amount of work can be avoided by limiting the calculation of the weighted average to the more current products in the group. Here the phenomenon known as Pareto's Law usually applies where from 10 to 20% of the number of types in a group will represent up to 80% or more of the total value of the group. If the calculation of the price index is based on this selected number of types, the outcome will almost always be reliable enough for decision-making purposes. The weighting should be based on the volume of the various types that is expected to be sold in the period for which the price index is prepared. If all types are sold in approximately the same proportion throughout the year, the simplest method is then to use the annual volume of sales, either actual or budgeted.

2.6 Standard Costs and Accounting

The use of standard costs, adjusted by price indices to reflect current values, can again best be demonstrated by means of an example:

> Assume that the merchandise of the business enterprise of the previous sections consisted of one group of products with a great variety of items, as for instance brass hardware. Based on a number of selected product types and the estimated volume of sales, price indices were calculated at the beginning of each three-month period to be used for that period. Since prices has been rising steadily for a longer period of time and the trend was still upwards, a certain degree of further advance was included in these indices; consequently the following price indices were set up for 1973:

1st quarter	102
2nd quarter	103
3rd quarter	105
4th quarter	108

With reference to the standard cost of sales, the current cost of sales was calculated as follows:

Quarter	Standard Cost of Sales	Index	Current Cost of Sales
1	$ 25,000	102	$ 25,500
2	25,000	103	25,750
3	25,000	105	26,250
4	25,000	108	27,000
Totals	$100,000		$104,500

We assume further that the inventories at the beginning of the year were valued at standard costs, which at that time were equal to the then current price level. Purchases in 1973 which actually cost $105,000 were valued at standard costs of $100,000. The inventory at year end amounted to $100,000 at standard costs and to $110,000 at current prices. As in earlier parts of this chapter it is assumed that the current value of the shareholders' equity has risen in the same proportions as the price index for goods, namely by 10%.

Purchase Price Variance Account

Under the application of standard costs the inventory account is kept at standard prices. Any differences between standard costs on the one hand and actual or current costs on the other hand are transferred to a "purchase price variance account." The inventory account appears as follows:

INVENTORY ACCOUNT 1973

Jan. 1 Balance: 10,000 at $10.00	$100,000	Dec. 31 Cost of sales: 10,000 at $10.00	$100,000
Dec. 31 Purchases: 10,000 at $10.00	100,000	Dec. 31 Balance: 10,000 at $11.00	110,000
Dec. 31 Revision of standard costs *	10,000		
	$210,000		$210,000

*It is assumed here that at year end the inventory on hand has been revalued at the revised standard cost prices which will apply in 1974; further it is assumed that the current price level and the new standard cost level were equal at year end.

The journal entries for purchases and cost of sales for 1973 are as follows:

Inventories	$100,000	
(purchases at standard costs)		
Purchase price variance account	5,000	
(for the difference between standard and actual costs)		
Cash		$105,000
(for the purchases at actual costs)		

and

Cost of sales	104,500	
(at current costs)		
Inventories		100,000
(at standard costs)		
Purchase price variance absorbed		4,500
(for the price index allowance)		

After these entries have been posted, the purchase price variance account shows a debit balance of $500 caused by the actual current costs having been slightly higher (5%) than the estimates included in the price indices (4.5%). Differences of this nature are unavoidable and provided they do not go beyond a reasonable tolerance, can be accepted as normal and be transferred to the profit and loss account. As long as the inventories do not fluctuate in volume during a period, the balance in the purchase price variance account provides a good check on the accuracy of the price indices used to calculate the current value of the cost of sales. The purchase price variance account in this example appears as follows:

PURCHASE PRICE VARIANCE ACCOUNT 1973

Dec. 31 On purchases	$ 5,000	Dec. 31 Absorbed by sales	$ 4,500
		Dec. 31 Loss	500
	$ 5,000		$ 5,000

The profit and loss account will now show two items:

Trading profit ($110,000 sales less $104,500 cost of sales)	$5,500
Unfavourable purchase price variance	500
Operating profit	$5,000

The balance sheet at year end will be exactly as in Section 2.2 above:

BALANCE SHEET AS AT DECEMBER 31, 1973

Inventory, at standard costs	$110,000	Equity:	
Cash	5,000	Original	$100,000
		Adjustment	10,000
		Current value	$110,000
		Operating profit	5,000
	$115,000		$115,000

2.7   Standard Costs and Fluctuating Inventories

Because inventories in the example in the previous section remained static throughout the year the cause of the balance in the purchase price variance account was exclusively due to an under-estimate of the amounts to be absorbed by means of the price indicies. If, however, the inventories fluctuate, as indicated in Section 2.3, the causes of a balance in the purchase price variance account become mixed. Since with care, the price indices can be calculated rather accurately, it may be safely assumed that a balance in the purchase price variance account at the end of a period in which the inventory has been fluctuating must be due to advanced or late buying.

Speculative Results

If the reason for this action is deliberate in order to take advantage of price fluctuations, for instance to buy in advance of the expected requirements of inventories when price increases are anticipated, or to delay the replacement of used inventories when prices are expected to decline, then a balance in the purchase price variance account should be qualified as a "speculative result" and need not be treated as part of the normal trading results.

The purchase price variance account, based on the delayed buying example of Section 2.3 at a purchase cost of $106,800 and the use of price indices as illustrated in the previous section, would then appear as follows:

PURCHASE PRICE VARIANCE ACCOUNT 1973

Dec. 31 On purchases	$ 6,800	Dec. 31 Absorbed by sales	$ 4,500
		Dec. 31 Loss	2,300
	$ 6,800		$ 6,800

We know from the previous section that $500 of the loss of $2,300 is due to an under-estimate of the price indices. In actual practice the breakdown of the $2,300 would not have been known, unless an elaborate and time-consuming analysis has been made to segregate the effects of the various causes. An intelligent estimate with respect to the main cause, as already suggested, is usually sufficient.

Accuracy in Accounting

In the process of valuation and income determination much is arbitrary. For that reason the best possible approximation of the values involved will be acceptable under most circumstances. This does not apply, of course, to the custodial aspects of accounting such as the accounting and control of cash and bank transactions, trade accounts and liabilities. Here accuracy is a necessity. In the areas of cost calculations, asset valuation and income determination, accuracy is a myth and as such can be a nuisance. *Reliability* based on a fair approximation of the data is what counts.

Chapter 3

ACCOUNTING SYSTEM IN TRADING ENTERPRISES (continued)

3.1 Monetary Assets and Current Values

The accounting system based on the current value concept will show that, in times of inflation, monetary or nominal assets generate a loss. For example:

The opening balance sheet of a merchandising company as at January 1, 1973 shows the following picture:

Assets

Inventory	$100,000
Accounts receivable	25,000
Cash	10,000
	$135,000

Shareholders' equity	$135,000

We further assume as in Section 2.1, that during 1973:

Purchases, total cost	$105,000
Sales, total proceeds	$110,000
Cost of sales amount to	$105,000
All transactions are on a cash basis, no expenses are taken into account and inventory stays at the same level in quantities throughout the year,	

and at the year end:

Inventory at current value amounts to	$110,000
Accounts receivable outstanding	$ 27,500
Current value of the original equity has risen by 10%	

After all entries have been posted, the revaluation adjustment account appears as follows:

REVALUATION ADJUSTMENT ACCOUNT 1973

Dec. 31 Revaluation of equity	$ 13,500	Dec. 31 Revaluation of inventory	$ 10,000
		Dec. 31 Loss	3,500
	$ 13,500		$ 13,500

The balance sheet at year end will appear:

BALANCE SHEET AS AT DECEMBER 31, 1973

Inventory	$110,000	Equity:	
Accounts receivable	27,500	Original	$135,000
		Revaluation	13,500
Cash	12,500	Current value	$148,500
		Profit*	1,500
	$150,000		$150,000

*Consisting of:	
Operating profit	$ 5,000
Revaluation loss	3,500
Profit	$ 1,500

The revaluation loss amounts to 10% of the equity funds invested in monetary assets as at the beginning of the year (accounts receivable $25,000 and cash $10,000).

From this example it may be concluded that the maximum amount of profit available for income taxes and for distribution to shareholders is $1,500. More cannot be paid out without affecting the shareholders' equity, and certainly, in the long run, without endangering the continuity of the enterprise on the same scale as before.

Unavoidable Inflation Losses are Costs

When *inflation losses* on the balance of nominal assets and liabilities are unavoidable and thus inherent in the business process, these losses should be considered as a *part of the normal cost* of the operation and be included in the standard operating costs. As a corollary of the above a company, in times of inflation, makes an *inflation profit* when the monetary liabilities exceed the monetary assets.

Holding Gains Concept Expanded

In the case of holding gains which emanate only from the revaluation of physical assets, the loss of purchasing power of the monetary assets would not be recorded as a loss. However, there is no objection to increasing the holding gains account by a sum to offset the loss of purchasing power of the monetary assets. This procedure is *imperative* if the available cash reserves originate from temporarily lower inventories or from accumulated amortization of fixed assets, in which case the cash involved is committed latently for replenishment of the inventories or replacement of the physical assets involved. In these circumstances, the continuity principle demands that the loss of purchasing power of the committed cash resources be deducted from the operating profit.

Financial Structure and Inflation

Inflation losses on monetary assets can be reduced or eliminated by arranging the financial structure of the enterprise in such a way that the monetary assets are partly or entirely offset by liabilities. Such arrangements may include buying on credit or financing part of the assets by borrowed capital instead of using equity capital for this purpose. The accountant should determine which financial structure is the optimal one for the enterprise. Borrowing at high interest rates, although alleviating the income tax burden, may well be more expensive than the cost of inflation in times of a lower rate of inflation. However, it is not the objective of this book to enter into a treatise on financing, a different subject that should be considered when organizing the financial structure of the enterprise and developing long range plans. The purpose of this chapter is restricted to showing how the accounting system operates in times of inflation under the application of the current value concept.

3.2 Difference Between Current Values of Assets and Equity

So far we have assumed that inflation, or whatever forces underly changes in prices, have the *same effect* on the *purchasing power of the dollar* as on the *prices of the commodities*. In actual practice inflation is only one force, albeit a strong one, behind ever-changing values. Prices of commodities, which include the cost of services and taxes, are affected not only by inflation but also by, among other things, technological changes, productivity increases, higher production volume, monopolistic tendencies, and political changes which in turn affect import duties and taxes. For these reasons the trends in the prices of various commodities do not necessarily run parallel; some may even be downward, while others may be up.

The implementation of the current value concept on the inventory of purchased goods at a specific date does not appear to present a problem; the *recent market price is the current value*. The more difficult question involves the way in which to assess the current value of the *shareholders' equity*. In Section 1.4 it was pointed out that two alternatives are available, which will be discussed here in more detail:

1. Value the equity to the same extent as the assets of the enterprise based on the *specific rate of inflation*.

2. Value the equity on the more universal basis of the *general rate of inflation* as expressed by the Consumer Price Index, or even better by using the GNE Implicit Price Index.

The two alternatives may provide different answers. The first solution harbors a risk if the company carries a product line that gradually becomes obsolete, such as pocket watches or fountain pens, which management attempts to counteract by diversification or by switching to other product lines. A sudden technological innovation may decrease the price of the product to a fraction of the previous price, as a result of which a greatly reduced equity capital would be adequate to continue the same activity as before. Possibly the equity should not be revalued downwards if it is expected that the lower cost of the commodity will bring about an increase in the sales volume to such an extent that the original equity should be conserved in order to enable the enterprise to handle the increased volume. In this case the adjustment of the inventory on hand to the reduced current prices must be taken as a loss.

The first alternative, that of relating the current value of the equity to the assets, does not seem to be such a good idea in a changing world, unless the enterprise, in its activities and product lines, is already so diversified that the upward-and-downward changes in the current values of its assets offset each other to such a degree that the balance of all the changes becomes manageable. For an enterprise of this nature its specific "equity index" may approach the general price indices mentioned in the second alternative.

The selection of the first alternative might imply that the primary objective of an enterprise is to remain static in those activities in which it is involved. Since the most important objective of an enterprise is to employ the equity capital to earn an inflation-proof income for the owners, management and personnel, the second alternative should prevail.

When differing price indices are applied to assets and to the shareholders' equity a variance may occur. The variance will be favourable when the amount by which the assets are revalued exceeds the amount by which the shareholders' equity is revalued, and vice-versa. To illustrate:

The assumptions are the same as in Section 3.1, but the shareholders' equity is adjusted on the basis of the Consumer Price Index which at year end in relation to January 1, 1973 amounts to 106.

After all entries have been posted, the revaluation adjustment account appears as follows:

REVALUATION ADJUSTMENT ACCOUNT 1973

Dec. 31 Revaluation of equity: 6% of $135,000	$ 8,100	Dec. 31 Revaluation of inventory	$ 10,000
Dec. 31 Variance	1,900		
	$ 10,000		$ 10,000

Character of the Revaluation Variance

What should be done with the favourable variance of $1,900? It could be taken into income, but considering that following years might show unfavourable variances if the general rate of inflation exceeded the rate of increase in asset values, it would be prudent to transfer a favourable variance to a special "revaluation reserve account" to offset possible future unfavourable variances. When no reserve is available, unfavourable variances should be charged off to the income account.

The balance sheet at year end now appears as follows:

BALANCE SHEET AS AT DECEMBER 31, 1973

Inventory	$110,000	Equity:	
Accounts receivable	27,500	Original	$135,000
		Revaluation 6%	8,100
Cash	12,500		
		Current value	$143,100
		Revaluation reserve	1,900
		Operating profit	5,000
	$150,000		$150,000

3.3 Variations in Current Values and Standard Costs at Year End Closing

In Section 2.6 it was assumed that at year end the inventories were revalued at the revised standard cost prices which would apply to next year's operations and further that these new standard cost prices were identical with the purchase prices at year end.

In actual practice, this would be a rare coincidence, due to the fact, as explained in Section 2.5, that revision of the standard costs generally begins well in advance of the year to which they will apply. Regardless of the price level upon which the new standard costs will be based, the current value of the inventories at year end will usually vary from the inventories at standard costs.

Inventory Price Level Adjustment Account

To solve this problem, assume that in Section 2.6 the current price level at year end, according to the latest price index calculation, appears to be 1% below the revised standard cost level. For this purpose a new account, "inventory prive level adjustment account," is used to record the difference between the inventories at standard costs and at current values. This amounts to $1,100 in our example, so the actual revaluation amounts to $8,900 ($10,000 standard cost revision less $1,100). The journal entry for the revision of standard cost prices in this case would be:

Inventories	$10,000	
Inventory price level adjustment account		$1,100
Revaluation adjustment account		8,900

The shareholders' equity in Section 2.2 was revalued by 10%, or $10,000. Accordingly we now have, as in Section 3.2, a *revaluation variance* due to the fact that the rise in current prices of the merchandise in which our enterprise was involved since the beginning of the year was different from the change in the price index used to revalue the equity. This is brought out in the accounting system by using the revaluation adjustment account, after the revaluation of the shareholders' equity has been booked with the following entry:

Revaluation adjustment account $10,000
    Shareholders' equity $10,000

After these entries have been made the revaluation adjustment account appears as follows:

REVALUATION ADJUSTMENT ACCOUNT 1973

Dec. 31 Revaluation of equity by 10%	$ 10,000	Dec. 31 Revaluation of inventory	$ 8,900
		Dec. 31 Loss transferred to profit and loss account	1,100
	$ 10,000		$ 10,000

The balance sheet at year end will appear:

BALANCE SHEET AS AT DECEMBER 31, 1973

Inventory, at standard costs	$110,000	Equity:	
Adjustments	1,100	Original	$100,000
Current value	$108,900	Revaluation	10,000
Cash	5,000	Current value	$110,000
		Operating profit*	3,900
	$113,900		$113,900

*Consisting of:
1. Tradng profit (See Section 2.6)		$5,500
2. Less:		
2.1 Revaluation adjustments	$1,100	
2.2 Unfavourable purchase price variance	500	1,600
Operating Profit		$3,900

Interim Closings

The procedure used in this section can be followed for interim (monthly, quarterly or half-yearly) closings. It can also be used when the books are closed off on the basis of the old standard costs and when the revised standard cost prices are introduced into the accounting records at the beginning of the period. In this case the journal entry on page 53 would be:

Inventory price level adjustment account	$ 8,900	
Revaluation adjustment account		$ 8,900
(for the difference between the inventories		
at current value of $108,900 and at old		
standard costs of $100,000)		

The item "Inventory" on the balance sheet at	
year end at the old standard costs would then be	$100,000
plus the difference with current prices	8,900
in total	$108,900

In January 1974 the new standard cost prices would be introduced in the accounts as follows:

Inventory	$10,000	
Inventory price level adjustment account		$ 10,000
(for the difference between the old and		
the new standard cost prices)		

After this entry the last-mentioned account would show a credit balance of $1,100, the same amount as per the earlier procedure.

3.4 Inventories Lower at Year End

When physical assets, such as inventories of merchandise which are more or less inflation-proof, are replaced by monetary assets in a time of rising prices, a loss is incurred as illustrated in the following example:

> Assume that in the example in Section 3.1, the purchases amount to $80,000 at standard costs and to $84,100 actual costs, as a result of which the year end inventory has decreased to $80,000 at standard costs. The other assumptions, such as the price index at year end, in terms of the old standard costs, is 109 for the merchandise and 110 for the shareholders' equity.

The effect is shown below:

PURCHASE PRICE VARIANCE ACCOUNT 1973

Dec. 31 On purchases	$ 4,100	Dec. 31 Absorbed in sales *		$ 4,500
Deo. 31 Profit trancferred to profit and loss account	400			
	$ 4,500			$ 4,500

*See Section 2.6.

Analysis of Variance

From the favourable balance in this account it would be incorrect to draw the conclusion that the price indices used to calculate the cost of sales have been on the high side. The favourable balance has been caused by the purchases having been lower than sales. It would require a further analysis to determine:

1. The deviation of the price indices from the actual current cost of sales. In Section 2.6 we observed that only when the inventories remain static over a period does the balance in the purchase price variance account provide a check on the accuracy of the price indices.

2. The profit or loss due to lower purchases. Since we know that actual current costs exceeded the estimates included in the price indices causing a loss of $500 (See Sections 2.6 and 3.3) when purchases of $100,000 at standard costs were made in 1973, then the profit due to lower purchases would be $900.

However, the profit is more than offset by the loss caused by the conversion of $20,000 of physical assets to monetary assets, which shows up in the revaluation adjustment account as follows:

REVALUATION ADJUSTMENT ACCOUNT 1973

Dec. 31 Revaluation of equity by 10%	$ 10,000	Dec. 31 Revaluation of inventory: 9% of $80,000	$ 7,200
		Dec. 31 Loss transferred to profit and loss account	2,800
	$ 10,000		$ 10,000

On the balance sheet at year end it will appear:

BALANCE SHEET AS AT DECEMBER 31, 1973

Inventory, at standard costs	$ 80,000	Equity: Original	$100,000
Adjustment	7,200	Revaluation	10,000
Current value	$ 87,200	Current value	$110,000
Cash	25,900	Operating profit *	3,100
	$113,100		$113,100

*Consisting of:
1. Trading profit		$ 5,500
2. Less the net of:		
2.1 Revaluation adjustments	$2,800	
2.2 Favourable purchase price variance	400	2,400
Operating Profit		$ 3,100

The $2,800 loss on the revaluation adjustment account can be analysed as follows:

1. A difference of one index point between the price
   index for equity (110) and for merchandise (109)
   on inventories of $80,000 at standard costs $ 800

2. A loss of 10 index points purchasing power on the
   $20,000 cash originally invested in inventories   2,000
                                                                  _____
                                                                   $2,800
                                                                  ========

The non-trading or extraordinary loss of $2,400 deducted from the regular trading profit could also be analysed as follows:

1. Unfavourable purchase price variance $ 500

2. A loss of one index point on the physical assets in
   comparison with the equity   800

3. A loss of $2,000 due to the conversion of physical
   assets to monetary assets during the year, less
   $900 due to lower purchases   1,100
                                                                  _____
                                                                   $2,400
                                                                  ========

The $1,100 in this example is less than 10% of the $20,000 increase in monetary assets since the conversion did not occur at the beginning of the year but, according to our assumptions, during the year.

Holding Gains Concept and Lower Inventories

If the company in this example had followed the holding gains concept explained in Section 1.4, the balance sheet at year end would have appeared as follows:

BALANCE SHEET AS AT DECEMBER 31, 1973

Inventory, at current value	$ 87,200	Equity	$100,000
Cash	25,900	Holding gains	9,000
		Operating profit	4,100
	$113,100		$113,100

The holding gains account would have been credited for:

1. The increase in value of the inventories $7,200

2. Less the net of:

2.1 The cash required to raise the inventories to the original (or normal) level at year end prices	$21,800	
2.2 The cash released by the reduction of the inventories since the beginning of 1973	20,000	1,800
Total		$9,000

The assumption here is that the continuity of the enterprise demands an inventory level of $100,000 expressed in terms of the price level at January 1, 1973, which in the language of the holding gains concept is defined as "normal level." It follows logically that $21,800 cash ($20,000 from the January 1, 1973 inventories at the year end price index of 109) is committed to the continuation of the enterprise and not available for distribution. This leaves a balance of $4,100 cash which in this example coincides with the operating profit of $4,100.

The operating profit under this concept consists of:

1. Trading profit		$5,500
2. Less the net of:		
2.1 Loss of purchasing power of the commited cash	$1,800	
2.2 Favourable purchase price variance	400	1,400
Operating profit		$4,100

The operating profit under this concept is $1,000 higher than under the equity concept based on the general rate of inflation, reflecting the fact that the inflation index applied to the equity (110) was 1 index point higher than the price index applied to the inventories and the committed part of the available cash. Under the other equity concept, based on the specific rate of inflation, the outcome would have been the same as in this example.

3.5   Inventories Higher at Year End

When the inventories at the end of the year are higher than at the beginning of the year the revaluation gain on the original inventory volume will be different from that on the additional volume. This must be taken into account when determining the operating results on one hand and the revaluation results on the other. To illustrate:

Assume that the inventories of the company in the previous section at year end amounted to $120,000 at standard costs; the purchases during the year amounted to $120,000 at standard costs and to $126,000 at actual costs. The other assumptions remain the same.

From this it follows that the additional inventory of $20,000 at standard costs was acquired, on the basis of an average inventory cost throughout the year, for $20,000 × $126,000 : $120,000 = $21,000. The $1,000 that was paid in excess of the standard costs must be taken into account by calculating the revaluation gains on the inventories at year end.

The current value of the inventories at year end based on a price index of 109 (See Section 3.4) amounts to $120,000 × 109 : 100 = $130,800, thus $10,800 higher than at the beginning of the year. The revaluation gain amounts to $10,800 less $1,000 paid in excess of standard costs for the additional inventory; accordingly, the revaluation amounts to $9,800.

The purchase price variance account would then appear as follows:

PURCHASE PRICE VARIANCE ACCOUNT 1973

Dec. 31 On purchases	$ 6,000	Dec. 31 Absorbed in sales	$ 4,500
		Dec. 31 Transfer to revaluation adjustment account	1,000
		Dec. 31 Loss transferred to profit and loss account	500
	$ 6,000		$ 6,000

And the revaluation adjustment account:

REVALUATION ADJUSTMENT ACCOUNT 1973

Dec. 31 Revaluation of equity by 10%	$ 10,000	Dec. 31 Revaluation of inventory: 9% of $120,000	$ 10,800
Dec. 31 Transfer from purchase price variance account	1,000	Dec. 31 Loss transferred to profit and loss account	200
	$ 11,000		$ 11,000

3.6   Obsolescence and Current Values

Thus far we have assumed that the current value of assets was identical with their *cost of replacement*. This supposition implied that the assets, after having been sold, would be replaced in due course, or at least could be replaced unless certain considerations prevented their timely replacement, such as the reduction of inventories on hand for lack of space or because of diminishing sales.

Frequently, however, the entire inventory is not sold in due course. In every enterprise a certain percentage of the products or materials become obsolete and must be sold at reduced prices or be scrapped. Sometimes the items involved can be replaced with something more modern but are discontinued for economic reasons. Other items are discontinued and the balance in stock must be disposed of. Manufacturing materials, components and sub-assemblies left over from previous production runs and not required for future production runs or for repairs are usually scrapped.

Inventory Valuation

What is the *current value* of inventories of this nature? Obviously, products or materials which are no longer used in producing the mainstream of revenue flowing into a business enterprise have likely depreciated in value and should not be valued at replacement cost. The valuation principle to be used here is: *the estimated proceeds less the costs to obtain these proceeds*, usually referred to as the *net proceeds*. Under the current value concept, the inventory valuation rule becomes *replacement cost and net proceeds, whichever is lower*. This is a variant to the conventional rule *cost and market, whichever is lower*.

Accounting Procedure for Obsolescence

The accounting procedure to record obsolescence for products and materials is more straightforward than for fixed assets. This subject is dealt with separately in Chapter 5, "Fixed Assets and Current Values." Differences between the prices at which the obsolete items appear in the records and the net proceeds (probable selling prices less selling expenses) should be written off in order to keep the assets at their current values in the accounts. Generally a certain amount of obsolescence is a normal and regular phenomenon in business. For this reason inventory write-offs of this nature should be considered as part of the normal cost of doing business. Under the standard cost concept an appropriate percentage of sales or cost of sales should be included in the standard costs to cover these write-offs. The relevant periodic journal entries would be:

Cost of sales	$xxxxx	
Provision for obsolete inventories		$xxxxx
(x% of sales)		

and each time that items are reduced in value because of obsolescence:

Provision for obsolete inventories	$xxxxx	
Inventories		$xxxxx
(for the write-off)		

Alternative Procedure

Sometimes it is more practical to book the write-off after the obsolete goods have been disposed of. This is the usual procedure for materials sold for scrap. If it is more convenient for accounting purposes, the same procedure could also be followed for the disposal of regular goods. The actual losses would be charged to the provision for obsolescence instead of charging the estimated write-offs prior to disposal. In this case a balance should be kept in the provision account to prevent overvaluation of the inventory.

Adjustment of Provision for Obsolescence

When the provision for obsolescence account shows a favourable balance after a period of some years, the balance should be adjusted to a lower level based on experience, and the excess over this level should be transferred to the profit and loss account as a favourable performance variance in the management of inventories. If a reduced write-off for obsolescence is apparently sufficient, consideration should be given to reducing the standard percentage.

However, if the provision account consistently shows an unfavourable balance due to higher write-offs than expected, this could mean that:
1. The degree of obsolescence was underestimated, or
2. Inventory management is less efficient than expected.

In both cases the unfavourable variance should be transferred to the profit and loss account as a performance variance, but with a note that the causes of the variance are different. In actual practice it is difficult if not impossible to segregate the two causes, unless one of the two is conspicuous. If it is evident that the degree of obsolescence is the main cause of the deficits in the provision account, the standard allowance should be raised.

3.7 Frequency of Value Adjustments

Current cost information, particularly on products and services, should be available at all times to enable management to set and review *at any time* its policies and decisions with respect to pricing sales, buying or making and similar day-to-day activities. This can be done either by adjusting the cost information itself or by using cost and price indices as discussed in Section 2.5.

The frequency of cost and price revisions depends on the nature of the business and on the rate and frequency of changes in costs and prices. For effective profit control, management must ensure that it is notified immediately of any change in current costs and prices which may significantly affect profit margins. Acceptable parameters should be established by management beyond which it must be informed; for example, more than 1% on purchased products held for resale and more than 2% for manufacturing materials.

With respect to a revision of the value of *fixed assets* and other assets which are not for sale as well as of the *shareholders' equity* an annual adjustment may suffice, unless the rate of inflation and price changes exceeds the 4 or 5% level. Since every system of valuation is to some extent arbitrary, depending not only on principles but also on conventions and rules which may be more or less subjective, it does not make much sense to create considerable work by demanding an adjustment of the assets and the equity each time prices have changed by 2 or 3%. The immediate effect on the profitability by changes of this magnitude is generally insignificant. Every enterprise has to establish its own limits beyond which a revision is deemed necessary.

Chapter 4

COMPARATIVE SUMMARY OF THE EFFECTS OF THE DIFFERENT CONCEPTS OF PROFIT

4.1 Introduction

In Section 1.4 it was explained that the different concepts under which the income available for distribution can be calculated lead to different answers. Since the holding gains concept is considered to be inferior to the equity concept in that it does not reflect the changes in the current value of the shareholders' equity, the subsequent chapters were based on the equity concept, either by using the general rate of inflation or the specific rate of inflation to arrive at a suitable price index for adjustment purposes.

At this point it is appropriate to review the effects of the different concepts on the balance sheet and on the distributable profit, under varying conditions. Using the figures from the examples in Section 1.4, the following illustrations show the effects of the different concepts when the company is:

1. Financed by equity funds only,

2. Financed by equity and other funds, creating an excess of liabilities over monetary assets, or has an

3. Excess of monetary assets over liabilities,

and, side by side, the effects of the different concepts in:

1. An ideal situation with respect to the level of the non-monetary assets.

2. A situation in which there is an amortization or inventory gap.

These illustrations are summarized in Section 4.5, a comparative schedule of profits under the various concepts and conditions.

4.2 Financed by Equity Funds Only

Inventories Unchanged				With Inventory Gap of 40%			
Historical Cost Concept				*Historical Cost Concept*			
Inventory	$105,000	Equity	$100,000	Inventory	$ 63,000	Equity	$100,000
Cash	5,000	Profit	10,000	Cash	47,000	Profit	10,000
	$110,000		$110,000		$110,000		$110,000

Current Value – Holding Gains Concept

Inventory	$110,000	Equity	$100,000
Cash	5,000	Holding gains	10,000
		Profit	5,000
	$115,000		**$115,000**

Current Value – Holding Gains Concept I

Inventory	$ 66,000	Equity	$100,000
Cash	47,000	Holding gains	8,000
		Profit	5,000
	$113,000		**$113,000**

Current Value – Holding Gains Concept II

Inventory	$ 66,000	Equity	$100,000
Cash	47,000	Holding gains *	10,000
		Profit	3,000
	$113,000		**$113,000**

*Revaluation of inventory	$8,000
Add: Provision for loss of purchasing power of cash committed for replenishment of inventory to normal level	2,000
	$10,000

Current Value – Equity Concept I
(*based on specific rate of inflation of 10%*)

Inventory	$110,000	Equity	$110,000
Cash	5,000	Profit	5,000
	$115,000		**$115,000**

Current Value – Equity Concept I
(*based on specific rate of inflation of 10%*)

Inventory	$ 66,000	Equity	$110,000
Cash	47,000	Profit	3,000
	$113,000		**$113,000**

Current Value – Equity Concept II
(*based on general rate of inflation of 12%*)

Inventory	$110,000	Equity	$112,000
Cash	5,000	Profit *	3,000
	$115,000		**$115,000**

*Operating profit		$5,000
Revaluation of:		
Equity by 12%	$12,000	
Inventory by 10%	10,000	
Revaluation deficit		2,000
Profit		**$3,000**

Current Value – Equity Concept II
(*based on general rate of inflation of 12%*)

Inventory	$ 66,000	Equity	$112,000
Cash	47,000	Profit *	1,000
	$113,000		**$113,000**

*Operating profit		$5,000
Revaluation of:		
Equity by 12%	$12,000	
Inventory	8,000	
Revaluation deficit		4,000
Profit		**$1,000**

4.3   Financed by Equity and Other Funds

| Inventories Unchanged | | | | With Inventory Gap of 40% | | | |

Historical Cost Concept

Inventory	$105,000	Equity	$ 50,000	Inventory	$ 63,000	Equity	$ 50,000
Cash	5,000	Creditors	50,000	Cash	47,000	Creditors	50,000
		Profit	10,000			Profit	10,000
	$110,000		$110,000		$110,000		$110,000

Current Value – Holding Gains Concept   *Current Value – Holding Gains Concept* I

Inventory	$110,000	Equity	$ 50,000	Inventory	$ 66,000	Equity	$ 50,000
Cash	5,000	Creditors	50,000	Cash	47,000	Creditors	50,000
		Holding gains	10,000			Holding gains	8,000
		Profit	5,000			Profit	5,000
	$115,000		$115,000		$113,000		$113,000

Current Value – Holding Gains Concept II

Inventory	66,000	Equity	$ 50,000
Cash	47,000	Creditors	50,000
		Holding gains*	10,000
		Profit	3,000
	$113,000		$113,000

*Based on the same calculation as under Section 4.2

Current Value — Equity Concept I

Inventory	$110,000	Equity	$ 55,000
Cash	5,000	Creditors	50,000
		Revaluation surplus *	5,000
		Profit	5,000
	$115,000		$115,000

Current Value - Equity Concept I

Inventory	$ 66,000	Equity	$ 55,000
Cash	47,000	Creditors	50,000
		Revaluation surplus *	5,000
		Profit	3,000
	$113,000		$113,000

*Although a real gain due to the financial structure, this gain is not available for distribution because it is committed to maintain the inventory at the normal level of 10,000 pieces.

*Revaluation of inventory
(see page 12) $8,000
Less:
Revaluation of equity   5,000

Gain due to financial structure $3,000
Since $110,000 is required to
replenish the inventory to a normal
level of 10,000 pieces, for which
only $108,000 (Equity $55,000;
Creditors $50,000; Revaluation
gain of $3,000) is available, an
amount should be retained from
the operating profit of   2,000

Bringing the revaluation surplus to $5,000

On the other hand, if the financial structure is arranged with the understanding that any seasonal increase in the inventory above a minimum level is to be financed by suppliers or short term loans, the revaluation surplus of $3,000 in this example may be considered to be a profit due to an inflationary gain on the liabilities and, as such, could be considered as available for distribution. A similar reasoning applies in case of an amortization gap, in which amortization of fixed assets are used to pay off loans (See Sections 1.4 and 5.5). A similar reasoning applies to the Holding Gains Concept II; here the profit available for distribution would then be calculated as $5,000, as under the Holding Gains Concept I.

Current Value – Equity Concept II *(based on general inflation rate of 12%)*			
Inventory	$110,000	Equity	$ 56,000
Cash	5,000	Creditors	50,000
		Revaluation surplus *	4,000
		Profit	5,000
	$115,000		$115,000

*Revaluation of:

Inventory by 10%	$10,000
Equity by 12%	6,000
Revaluation surplus	$ 4,000

This amount is committed to inventories and thus not available for distribution.

Current Value – Equity Concept II *(based on general inflation rate of 12%)*			
Inventory	$ 66,000	Equity	$ 56,000
Cash	47,000	Creditors	50,000
		Revaluation surplus *	4,000
		Profit	3,000
	$113,000		$113,000

*Revaluation of:

Inventory	$8,000
Equity by 12%	6,000
Revaluation surplus	$2,000

Add:

Provision for replenishment of inventory to normal level, to be charged to operating profit	2,000
Revaluation surplus retained	$4,000

In case the inventory gap is seasonal (see the remark above under Equity Concept I) the revaluation gain of $4,000 may be considered as a profit and available for distribution.

4.4   Excess of Monetary Assets Over Liabilities

Inventories Unchanged	With Inventory Gap of 40%

Historical Cost Concept

Inventory	$105,000	Equity	$120,000
Accounts receivable	20,000	Profit	10,000
Cash	5,000		
	$130,000		$130,000

Historical Cost Concept

Inventory	$ 63,000	Equity	$120,000
Accounts receivable	20,000	Profit	10,000
Cash	47,000		
	$130,000		$130,000

Current Value – Holding Gains Concept

Inventory	$110,000	Equity	$120,000
Accounts receivable	20,000	Holding gains	10,000
Cash	5,000	Profit	5,000
	$135,000		$135,000

Current Value – Holding Gains Concept I

Inventory	$ 66,000	Equity	$120,000
Accounts receivable	20,000	Holding gains	8,000
Cash	47,000	Profit	5,000
	$133,000		$133,000

Current Value – Holding Gains Concept II

Inventory	$ 66,000	Equity	$120,000
Accounts receivable	20,000	Holding gains*	10,000
Cash	47,000	Profit	3,000
	$133,000		$133,000

*This amount may be further increased by $2,000 for a 10% loss of purchasing power on accounts receivable, reducing the profit available for distribution to $1,000.

Current Value – Equity Concept I
(based on specific rate of inflation of 10%)

Inventory	$110,000	Equity	$132,000
Accounts receivable	20,000	Profit *	3,000
Cash	5,000		
	$135,000		$135,000

*Operating profit		$5,000
Revaluation of:		
Equity by 10%	$12,000	
Inventory by 10%	10,000	
Revaluation deficit		2,000
Profit available for distribution		$3,000

Current Value – Equity Concept I
(based on specific rate of inflation of 10%)

Inventory	$ 66,000	Equity	$132,000
Accounts receivable	20,000	Profit *	1,000
Cash	47,000		
	$133,000		$133,000

*Operating profit		$5,000
Revaluation of:		
Equity by 10%	$12,000	
Inventory	8,000	
Revaluation deficit		4,000
Profit available for distribution		$1,000

Current Value – Equity Concept II
(based on general inflation rate of 12%)

Inventory	$110,000	Equity	$134,400
Accounts receivable	20,000	Profit *	600
Cash	5,000		
	$135,000		$135,000

*Operating profit		$5,000
Revaluation of:		
Equity by 12%	$14,400	
Inventory by 10%	10,000	
Revaluation deficit		4,400
Profit available for distribution		$ 600

Current Value – Equity Concept II
(based on general inflation rate of 12%)

Inventory	$ 66,000	Equity	$134,400
Accounts receivable	20,000		
Cash	47,000		
Loss *	1,400		
	$134,400		$134,400

*Operating profit		$5,000
Revaluation of:		
Equity by 12%	$14,400	
Inventory	8,000	
Revaluation deficit		6,400
Loss		$1,400

4.5 Comparative Summary of Profits under Various Concepts and Conditions

Concept and Application	Financed by Equity Funds		Excess of Liabilities over Monetary Assets		Excess of Monetary Assets over Liabilities	
	No Gap	Gap*	No Gap	Gap*	No Gap	Gap*
1. Historical Cost	$10,000	$10,000	$10,000	$10,000	$10,000	$10,000
2. Current Value, based on specific rate of inflation:						
2.1 Holding Gains Concept						
I. Only on physical assets	5,000	5,000	5,000	5,000	5,000	5,000
II. Plus provision for gap		3,000		3,000		3 000
III. Plus provision for purchasing power loss on accounts receivable				5,000		1,000
2.2 Equity Concept						
I. Plus provision for gap, if necessary	5,000	3,000	5,000	3,000	3,000	1,000
II. Gap is seasonal				8,000		
3. Current Value, based on general rate of inflation:						
3.1 Equity Concept						
I. Plus provision for gap, if necessary	3,000	1,000	5,000	3,000	600	(1,400)
II. Gap is seasonal				7,000		

*Inventory or amortization gap.

Chapter 5

FIXED ASSETS AND CURRENT VALUES

5.1 Land

Land should appear in the balance sheet at current value. With the exception of a few instances where market prices are readily available for similar parcels of land, the current value will have to be based on an estimate or appraisal of the probable market value.

But how should land be treated in the income account? What is the cost of land? Of course, there are property taxes and maintenance costs, but not amortization of the invested funds for wear and tear as with buildings and machinery and equipment, except in the rare event that the market value of the land diminishes for some reason. And yet, the most important ongoing cost in connection with land, the interest on the capital invested, is generally omitted in the conventional accounting rules. This brings us to the *principle of interest as part of the current value concept*.

5.2 Interest as a Cost Item

Interest is the *price for the capital funds* needed to buy facilities and goods. Capital funds, or purchasing power, are invested in these assets. The cost of the use of these funds is not the dividend a company pays to its shareholders and the interest a company pays for its borrowings, but rather the *current value of the use of these funds in an alternative process of making an income*; for example, investment in government or industrial bonds. The income from this alternative investment, which is foregone or given up by operating a merchandising, manufacturing or service enterprise, constitutes the *cost of using* the required funds, or *interest*. As with certain other costs, such as labour and rent, interest is *time-related* in that the interest is expressed in a percentage per year. Thus the interest cost in dollars depends on the *amount* of capital funds devoted to the operation as well as the *length of time* involved. Basically, the interest cost is an "opportunity" cost.

This is the *principle of interest* as one of the cost factors, regardless of whether the company is financed by equity capital or by loans or by both, and regardless of whether the company pays its shareholders a dividend or not. The latter belongs to the area of *financing policy*. A company may not pay a dividend to its shareholders in order to have cash available to amortize its loans or to finance business expansion. It may happen that a company is entirely financed by equity capital and that for some reason no dividend is paid out at all. As mentioned in Section 1.4, there is a difference between *income determination* and *income appropriation*, the first being one of the subjects of this book.

Financial Results and Residual Income

The principle of interest brings about a requirement for a new account called "financial results," to show on one hand the amount of interest charged to the cost of operations and on the other hand the actual interest paid on loans, dividends paid to shareholders and the income tax payable. The balance is sometimes called "residual income."

Section 1.5, dealing with the concept of current costs in general terms, touched on the principle of the imputed interest charged, and illustrated how to calculate a standard rate as an average of loan interest, a normative dividend as well as the income tax involved in a normative dividend. The question arises of *which* interest rates to use, the actual rates or the current rates. With respect to short term financing by means of bank demand loans or bank overdrafts, the actual rates coincide with the current rates. For long term loans, the actual rates may vary considerably from the current rates for similar loans. In principle the current rates should be used, as a result of which the above-mentioned "financial results" account will include an interest variance due to the actual rates being higher or lower than the current rates.

Practical Advantages of Imputed Interest Charges

Apart from the principle of an interest charge to the costs, there are some practical reasons for including interest in the costs, such as:

1. Interest expresses the relative importance of the capital funds devoted to the various operations as compared with the other cost factors. For instance, the interest charge for capital-intensive operations would be considerably higher than for labour-intensive operations.

2. Interest charges, as mentioned under Point 1, permit a more reliable measurement of the relative economy of various methods of operations.

3. Comparison of the cost of making or buying and the cost of owning or renting facilities would lead to incorrect conclusions without including interest charges.

4. Interest permits proper comparison and control of the profitability of various divisions, product groups, regions, and the like.

5. Interest promotes economy in the application of funds in facilities, inventories and trade accounts receivable.

A Case Study of High Land Costs

Some companies conduct their operations from expensive sites in highly built-up and congested downtown areas. If these companies would include an interest charge in their operating costs at the currently high rates for long term funds, based on the current value of the land occupied, it might provide them with an inducement to move to a location with lower land costs, assuming the cost of the move would be favorably offset by the present value of the expected savings in operating costs. To illustrate:

Assume that the current value of a plant, based on the principle of continuity, is as follows:

Land	$2,000,000
Buildings less amortization	250,000
Machinery and equipment less amortization	500,000
	$2,750,000

The company can sell the land for $2,000,000 net to a buyer who wants to use the land, after clearing, for a high-rise office building.

A new site could be purchased for	$100,000
on which a new plant could be built for	$700,000
The machinery and equipment can be moved to the new building.	
The total cost of the move, including salaries, wages and overheads during the time of the move are estimated at	$250,000

The operating costs at another location, in addition to higher amortization charges, are expected to rise by approximately $25,000 per year.

The additional costs of a new location, without an interest charge, namely:

1. Higher amortization charges (at 3% of the purchase price of the new building) per year	$ 21,000
2. Higher operating costs per year	25,000
Total per year	$ 46,000

do not seem to justify the cost of a move.

However, the inclusion of interest at 10% of the relevant market values changes the picture. The annual interest charge of the new location would be (10% of $800,000)	80,000
bringing the total additional yearly costs of the new location up to	$126,000
The annual interest charge of the present location would be (10% of the $2,000,000 market value of the present site including buildings).	200,000
resulting in a net annual saving of	$ 74,000

The present value of these savings, over a period of 10 years on the basis of 10% per year, would amount to $450,000, which amply justifies the cost of the move. The same conclusion would be reached by realizing that the cost of the move would be earned back in just over 3 years.

5.3   Buildings, Machinery and Equipment

Cost Classification

Generally, the cost of operations may be classified into three distinctive groups:

1. *Services by people,* labour cost and services rendered by outside private enterprises and public institutions.

2. *Materials* for resale, manufacturing, maintenance and other purposes.

3. *Contributions by facilities,* land, buildings and machinery and equipment.

A fundamental difference exists between the first two categories of costs and the last one. Since materials can be used only once in an operation, they should be replaced immediately in order to safeguard the continuity of the enterprise by being available for ensuing operations. Services are paid for, sometimes on a weekly, monthly or annual basis, when rendered.

Contribution Units

Facilities can be used repeatedly for a long time. From an operational and costing viewpoint they constitute an aggregate number of identical *contribution units or service units* which have to be purchased collectively. Sometimes this type of service can be bought per unit or per hour by subcontracting certain operations with other firms; sometimes it can be rented or leased, thereby avoiding capital investment. This will certainly happen when the typical services are only temporarily or occasionally required. If, however, these services are to be used in a certain volume for a longer period of time it may be more economical to buy them collectively. To illustrate:

> Assume that a certain operation, for example silverplating, can be performed by outsiders for $10 per hour. A machine that does the same job can be purchased for $25,000 and is capable of producing 1,500 hours per year during its estimated lifetime of 10 years. The additional cost to operate this machine (labour, power, maintenance, space and other costs) amounts to $6 per hour. It follows that the value of one hour's production of the machine is $4. The present value of these contributions over a period of 10 years, at an interest rate of 10% per year amounts to, according to the compound interest tables:
> $$6.144567 \times 1,500 \times \$4 = \$36,868$$
> Since the cost of the machine is lower, the purchase is justified.

Interest must be included in the calculation of the hourly cost for two reasons. It permits the continuous comparison of the company's own costs with those quoted by outsiders. Also this comparison can provide a basis for the valuation of the balance of remaining contributions of the machine. The latter point will be discussed further in Section 5.6.

5.4 Cost Per Contribution Unit and Asset Valuation

The cost of a contribution unit or a service unit of a production asset, such as a machine or a building, apart from the additional cost as previously mentioned, consists of amortization of the capital investment and the interest over the diminishing balance of the investment. The total cost divided by the number of contribution units, for instance hours or square feet of floor space, is the cost per unit.

Annuity Method of Amortization

There are many amortization or depreciation methods; some are very simple, others are complicated. One of these, the annuity method, recognizes the interest factor and provides that the *sum of amortization and interest is equal* for each year of the lifetime of an asset. For example:

The purchase price of a machine including installation costs is $25,000. The machine has an estimated useful lifetime of 10 years after which the machine will be scrapped. The amortization of the capital invested will be based on the annuity method with an interest rate of 10% per year. According to the annuity tables the 10-year 10% annuity is $0.162745 per $1, so for $25,000 the annuity is $4,068.63 or $4,069 rounded off. From this the following table can be prepared:

Year	Balance at Beginning of Year	Interest at 10% on Balance	Amortization $4,069 less Interest	Balance at Year End
1	$25,000	$2,500	$1,569	$23,431
2	23,431	2,343	1,726	21,705
3	21,705	2,171	1,898	19,807
4	19,807	1,981	2,088	17,719
5	17,719	1,772	2,297	15,422
6	15,422	1,543	2,526	12,896
7	12,896	1,290	2,779	10,117
8	10,117	1,012	3,057	7,060
9	7,060	706	3,363	3,697
10	3,697	370	3,697	—

The journal entry at the end of the first year would be as follows:

Machinery and equipment costs	$4,069	
Financial results		$2,500
(for the imputed interest charge)		
Accumulated amortization		1,569
(for the first year's amortization)		

If in subsequent years the price level remains unchanged, the charge to "machinery and equipment costs" will be $4,069 for each of the remaining nine years. Only the breakdown into the two factors of interest and amortization will be different each year. In actual practice these entries are generally made on a monthly basis, taking $\frac{1}{12}$ of the annual amounts collectively for all fixed assets. In larger companies they are broken down by division or departments. The individual asset accounts in the sub-ledger for fixed assets can be updated at year end.

Variant of the Annuity Method

A simplified variant of the annuity method is *straight line amortization plus interest on 60% of the purchase price of the asset.* Applied to the example above, this variant would show:

1. An annual amortization of $\frac{1}{10}$	$2,500
2. An annual interest charge of 10% on 60% of $25,000	1,500
Total "annuity"	$4,000

The resultant figure is slightly less than the theoretically more accurate figure produced by using the annuity method, but since both the cost and the valuation of the asset are based on an arbitrary estimate of the useful lifetime, the difference is of little importance. An advantage of this variant is that it simplifies considerably the accounting procedure, particularly the postings to the fixed assets sub-ledger.

When the annuity table is used, the current value of the asset is at all times the present value of the unused contributions as represented by the balance at year end in the previous table. Although the cost is the same each year when the above-mentioned simplified variant is used, the asset value is somewhat lower during the entire lifetime of the machine. This is shown by comparing the two valuation methods:

Asset Value at Year End	Annuity Method	Straight Line Method
1	$23,431	$22,500
2	21,705	20,000
3	19,807	17,500
4	17,719	15,000
5	15,422	12,500
6	12,896	10,000
7	10,117	7,500
8	7,060	5,000
9	3,697	2,500
10	—	—

5.5 Valuation of Fixed Assets when Price Level Changes

As long as the price level remains *static*, the annual or monthly charges to the cost accounts remain the same, and the unamortized part of the investment may be assumed to represent the current value of the asset, based on the replacement costs of identical assets less the accumulated amortization. But when the price level changes the charges to the cost accounts have to be adjusted accordingly. Assume that the price of the machine in the previous section rises in the 4th year by 10%. This increases the annuity calculation from $4,069 to $4,476, and the journal entry for the 4th year would be:

Machinery and equipment costs	$4,476	
Financial results		$2,179
(for the interest, $1,981 + 10%)		
Accumulated amortization		2,297
(for the 4th year amortization, $2,088 + 10%)		

When standard costs are in use, the higher machine costs would be included in the cost index of the products made with the machines involved.

Amortization Gap

The effect of the price increase may be that the company has to take a loss due to the fact that the amounts amortized in previous years, plus the expected amortization during the remaining years of the assets, is inadequate to provide sufficient cash to replace the assets involved. The two following balance sheets will illustrate this point. We assume that the company has only the above-mentioned machine which is now 4 years old.

BALANCE SHEET BEFORE REVALUATION

Machinery and equipment	$ 25,000	Equity	$ 25,000
Accumulated amortization	7,281	Profit for current year	2,000
Net book value	$ 17,719		
Cash	9,281		
	$ 27,000		$ 27,000

Assuming a price increase of 10% for assets as well as for the equity, the balance sheet after the revaluation would appear as follows:

BALANCE SHEET AFTER REVALUATION

Machinery and equipment, at replacement cost	$ 27,500	Equity: Original		$ 25,000
Accumulated amortization	8,009	Revaluation		2,500
Net book value at current price level	$ 19,491	Current value		$ 27,500
Cash	9,281	Profit:		
		Current year	$2,000	
		Loss on revaluation	728	
		Available for distribution		1,272
	$ 28,772			$ 28,772

The journal entries for this revaluation are as follows:

Machinery and equipment	$2,500	
Accumulated amortization		$ 728
Revaluation adjustment account		1,772
Revaluation adjustment account	2,500	
Shareholders' equity		2,500
Profit and loss account	728	
Revaluation adjustment account		728
(transfer of the loss)		

The loss of $728 represents the "amortization gap" of the past four years. The company must assume the *amortization arrears as a loss* and deduct this from the amount of profit available for distribution in order to save the cash which in due course will be required to replace the machine after it has become worn out or obsolete. Assuming that the price remains static during the last six years of the estimated lifetime of the machine, in this case $19,491, being the book value at the beginning of the six year period, will be amortized and turned into cash. After 10 years the $7,281 cash from the regular amortization during the first four years, plus $728 adjustment taken out of profit, together with $19,491 amortization during the last six years, makes a total of $27,500, which matches the replacement cost of the new machine.

Cost Allowance for Losses on Monetary Assets

The enterprise in this example is in the same position as the one in Section 3.1, where a loss was suffered in a period of rising prices on that part of the equity devoted to monetary assets. If losses of this nature are unavoidable they should be offset by an allowance in the operation costs.

Ideal Complex of Fixed Assets

In older companies of some size, where fixed assets were acquired gradually over the years and there is a fairly equal distribution with respect to ages, it may happen that the annual amortization on the basis of current values is approximately equal to the purchases of new capital assets. All capital assets together constitute an "ideal complex." The following example illustrates this point:

Assume that a company has 5 machines, the current price of which is $10,000 each; the estimated life of each is 5 years and the residual value after 5 years is nil. The ages are ideally distributed with the oldest machine having been bought 5 years ago and the newest one a year ago. Each year the oldest machine is scrapped and replaced by a similar machine. It is further assumed that the investment in the machines is amortized according to the straight line method. At each year end the following summary can then be prepared:

Age	Current Price	Amortization Each Year	Accumulated	Book Value at Year End
1	$10,000	$ 2,000	$ 2,000	$ 8,000
2	10,000	2,000	4,000	6,000
3	10,000	2,000	6,000	4,000
4	10,000	2,000	8,000	2,000
5	10,000	2,000	10,000	
Total	$50,000	$10,000	$30,000	$20,000

The last machine which is 5 years old will now be scrapped and replaced by a new machine, the current price of which is $10,000, equal to the annual amount of amortization for all 5 machines. Enterprises with their fixed assets in this position do not suffer losses from amortization arrears when the price level rises. Abstracted from everything else, the balance sheet before revaluation would appear as follows:

BALANCE SHEET BEFORE REVALUATION

Machinery and equipment	$ 50,000	Equity	$ 20,000
Accumulated amortization	30,000		
Net book value	$ 20,000		
	$ 20,000		$ 20,000

And after revaluation by 10%

BALANCE SHEET AFTER REVALUATION

Machinery and equipment	$ 55,000	Equity:	
Accumulated amortization	33,000	Original	$ 20,000
Net current value	$ 22,000	Adjustment	2,000
		Current value	$ 22,000
	$ 22,000		$ 22,000

Financing Fixed Assets to Avoid Losses

Another method to avoid or at least minimize losses caused by amortization gaps is to finance the fixed assets as much as possible with borrowed funds, unless the cost of borrowing is prohibitive. Assume that the company earlier in this section with the one $25,000 machine would have been financed not with $25,000 equity capital but with an equity of $10,000 and a loan of $15,000. The revaluation adjustment account would then have appeared as follows:

REVALUATION ADJUSTMENT ACCOUNT

Dec. 31 Revaluation of equity	$ 1,000	Dec. 31 Revaluation of machinery and equipment	$ 1,772
Dec. 31 Profit on revaluation	772		
	$ 1,772		$ 1,772

Instead of a revaluation loss of $728 there is now a revaluation profit of $772, a difference of $1,500, which represents 10% of the loan. If equity capital is scarce, the company would probably have no choice as to the method of financing, but if equity capital is available the loan interest burden must be weighed against the reward the shareholders forego. The policy of financing capital assets with borrowed funds, apart from cost and tax considerations, is justified as long as the company can raise the necessary funds at the time the assets involved must be replaced.

5.6 Replacement Prices Not Available or Not Applicable

Frequently market prices for new identical capital assets are *not available* because older types have been succeeded by more modern types or altogether different types of capital assets. Then the best solution to the valuation of the company's assets is to follow the trend in the market prices of the particular group of assets involved and each time a change of any significance (say 5% or more) is observed, to revalue the assets by using a price index to be equally applied to all assets of the group.

The valuation process becomes more complicated when valuation on the basis of replacement costs is *no longer applicable* since:

1. Replacement of the assets is not intended; for instance, as soon as the present assets are worn out, they will be replaced by leased assets or the old process will be replaced by a new process requiring different equipment.

2. Replacement of the assets is not economical; it is cheaper to have the particular operation performed by outside firms.

Even when replacement costs are available, either for each item or in the form of a price index, they do not apply to the two above-mentioned cases unless another valuation would lead to a higher value, in which case replacement cost being the lower, would prevail.

Future Proceeds as Basis of Valuation

The other valuation is based on the *future revenues* of the assets involved. The present value of all future proceeds less the cost to obtain those proceeds constitutes the economic value or current value of the assets involved. An illustration may help to explain this valuation principle:

The work performed by the $25,000 machine in Section 5.3 can now be performed by an outside firm for $7.50 per hour. Therefore, one hour's work on the company's own machine has an economic or return value of $1.50 ($7.50 less $6.00 for the additional cost). The machine is 4 years old and can be expected to last another 6 years. The book value is now $17,719.

On the basis of 1,500 productive hours per year during 6 years, the *present value* at an interest rate of 10% per year amounts to:

4.355621 × 1,500 × $1.50 = $9,800.15 or $9,800 rounded off

Since current value is $7,919 less than the book value, the difference should be written off. The 6-year 10% annuity for $9,800 is 0.229607 × $9,800 = $2,250, equalling exactly the annual return on the machine of $2,250 (1,500 × $1.50).

The above example explains in elementary terms the *valuation principle based on future revenues*. The application of this principle in actual practice is generally very difficult, but to be aware of the principle is a first step on the road to an improved valuation system.

The most difficult point is to establish the future revenues of the assets, which are required to determine their earning power or, in other words, the economic value of the contribution units. Many assets, particularly in manufacturing processes, are complementarily employed. In these cases only the revenues of the whole group can be determined, but not those of its parts. For all practical purposes the appropriate solutions are to base the valuation on the future proceeds of either the entire group if possible, or to apply the "index method" to the individual parts of the group.

Lifetime Variances

For costing purposes *the cost accounts should be charged* for the contribution of the assets *as long as they are usefully employed*; sometimes this may be longer, sometimes shorter than the estimated lifetimes of the assets. As soon as the current book value has been amortized completely, the full annuity, now consisting of an amortization factor only since the interest has become nil, should be credited to an "amortization variance account" or a "fixed assets lifetime variance account."

The book value less the residual value (realizable value or scrap value) of assets that have been put out of operation before reaching their estimated lifetimes should be written off against the above-mentioned variance account. Over a longer period of time the size of the balance in this variance account will indicate whether the useful lifetimes have, on the average for all capital assets, been estimated correctly. If the lifetimes have been over-estimated this will be signalled by a growing deficit balance in the variance account, and vice-versa. A revision of the estimated lifetimes may eventually be needed.

Chapter 6

MANUFACTURING OPERATIONS AND SERVICES UNDER THE CURRENT VALUE CONCEPT

6.1 Advantages of Standard Costs in Manufacturing

Maintaining a current value system in manufacturing enterprises is more difficult than in trading enterprises, as more cost factors are involved, such as the cost of labour, amortization of capital assets and a greater variety of other costs. With an integrated process, where successive operations are involved and transfer prices are required to record the flow of goods through various departments, the task of keeping management continuously informed about the current price levels may become cumbersome.

The use of a standard cost system may prove to be valuable, providing that a suitable type of standard costs is used. The well-known *Cost Accountants' Handbook*[1] mentions four types of standard costs: current, basic, ideal and normal standards, each of which can be differentiated further with respect to price levels, performance levels and activity levels. For the purpose at hand the most suitable type of standard costs would be the one that approaches as closely as possible the current value or replacement cost concept. Although other standard cost systems with the aid of adjustment indices would serve this purpose, the most desirable type of standard costs to represent the replacement cost concept is the type based on the two principles of *continuity* and *normality*; that is, costs based on:

1. Normal quantities of materials, time and services.

2. Normal operating conditions.

3. Normal performance by men and equipment, at a

4. Normal activity level.

This concept of standard costs, whether more or less scientifically pre-determined by a careful selection of materials, time and motion studies, etc. which greatly depends on the size of the company and the economics of such studies, provides the best conceivable answer to the question: "What does it cost to replace (reproduce) this product?" Under normal operating conditions standard costs are full costs including fixed overhead costs. Special cases, where differential or direct costs may be applicable, will be touched upon briefly in Chapter 8. For the purposes of asset valuation and costing we assume standard costs to be full costs. As long as the level of prices, wages and services upon which the standard costs are based does not change, the standard cost prices as defined above and current values are identical.

The use of standard costs as a basis for calculating the current costs with the aid of cost and price indices is not absolutely necessary. It is quite feasible, certainly in rather simple manufacturing processes, to apply indices to a base price or a base cost, for instance, the prices or costs at the beginning of the year. As a matter of fact this is exactly the way in which the Consumer Price Index is calculated.

6.2   Price Level Changes in Manufacturing

Two ways to cope with a change in price levels were described in Section 2.5:

1. A complete revision of the standard costs.

2. Use of a price index to adjust the standard costs to the new price level.

The first approach is quite feasible in companies with a limited number of products, where the up-dating can be done without a great deal of work. There is one objection to this procedure, stemming from the fact that standard costs are designed not only for valuation purposes but also for *performance control*. Since performance control is predominantly a quantitative process brought about by comparing actual quantities of materials used and actual operating time with the standard quantities, there is no necessity to change the price basis of the standard costs for this purpose. The conclusions about factory performance drawn from the variations from standard (for instance, a favourable or unfavourable time variance) would not be different if the variance were valued at a slightly higher or lower rate than the standard rate per hour. The choice of the approach to be followed is largely dictated by which is the more economical. In most cases the use of price indices will turn out to be the most efficient of the two.

If the system of price indices is chosen, the easiest accounting procedure is then to "screen off" the operations from the external price level changes. The entire operation, including the input of materials, time and other costs as well as the output of products or services, is recorded at standard cost prices. The differences between the actual costs and the standard costs are then recorded in price variance accounts whereas the index adjustments to the standard costs of the output (deliveries) are recorded in absorption accounts. The balance of the variance and absorption accounts together provides a check to what extent the price indices have been correct.

6.3   Calculation of Price Indices

As explained in Section 2.5 the price indices can be set on the basis of:

1. A weighted average of those product types which are representative for the group to which they belong, or

2. A prototype.

The first procedure takes more time than the second one and should be applied only when a prototype cannot be found in a product group.

In selecting the prototype method, the price index can be established either by:

1. Completely recalculating all cost factors of the prototype in all details as originally done for its standard cost price using the bill of materials, work instructions, and other cost data, or

2. First preparing prices indices for homogeneous groups of
    2.1 Materials, for example for iron, steel, copper, wood and such which are subject to similar price changes
    2.2 Direct labour
    2.3 Other costs,

and subsequently calculating, with the aid of these partial indices, a total price index for the prototype.

Example 1

The details that would appear in applying the first method are set out in the following table:

In $ per 100	Standard Cost	Current Cost	Index
Direct material costs	$147	$163	111
Material overheads	19	20	105
Machine costs	42	45	107
Direct labour	225	245	109
Factory overheads	227	240	106
Sub-total	$660	$713	108
Allowance for shrinkage 5%	35	38	—
Total	$695	$751	108

Example 2

The final part of the calculation of the price index, based on a prototype and on a number of partial price indices for each of the cost classifications having their own price level change, may be illustrated as follows:

	Standard Cost	Current Cost	Index
Direct material:			
Group A	$ 60.00	$ 63.60	106
Group B	20.00	20.00	100
Group C	10.00	10.50	105
Group D	10.00	10.70	107
Sub-total	$100.00	$104.80	105
Direct labour	$ 50.00	$ 51.50	103
Factory overhead costs:			
Salaries, indirect wages	$ 20.00	$ 20.40	102
Services	12.00	12.60	105
Amortization of interest on fixed assets	10.00	10.50	105
Other costs	8.00	8.00	100
Sub-total	$ 50.00	$ 51.50	103
Total	$200.00	$207.80	104

This method is quite useful and efficient for secondary industries, particularly those with products which involve a long bill of materials and undergo a variety of successive operations.

6.4   Application of Price Indices in Manufacturing

This section shows how the accounting system can be adapted to integrate both standard costs and current values in such a way that both the balance sheet and the income statement are the result of one accounting procedure.

BALANCE SHEET AT BEGINNING OF PERIOD

Machinery and equipment	$ 500,000	Equity	$ 500,000
Accumulated amortization	250,000	8% Loan	600,000
Net current value	$ 250,000	Accounts payable	200,000
Inventories:*			
Materials	$ 200,000		
Finished products	200,000		
	$ 400,000		
Accounts receivable	$ 270,000		
Cash	380,000		
	$1,300,000		$1,300,000

* The inventories are valued at standard costs which are identical with current costs at the beginning of the period.

The following transactions ensue during the period:

1. Purchases of materials, at actual costs $260,000
   at standard costs   250,000

2. Materials consumption by factory, at standard costs $235,000

3. Direct labour, at actual rates $130,000
   at standard rates   125,000

4. Factory overhead costs, at actual costs $131,000
   including: amortization of fixed assets   5,000
            and interest charge on fixed assets and inventories   3,000
   Factory overhead costs, at standard costs   125,000

5. Deliveries by the factory to the finished products stores:
   $480,000 at standard costs, broken down into

Materials	$240,000
Direct labour	120,000
Overhead costs	120,000
Total	$480,000

6. Sales $700,000
   Standard cost of sales   500,000

7. Selling expenses, actual costs $110,000
   including interest charge on inventories and accounts
       receivable   4,500
   Selling expenses at budgeted rate of 15%   105,000

8. Collected from customers $650,000
   Paid to suppliers   300,000
   Interest on loan   4,000

The price index for this period was set 104 (see Section 6.3), broken down into:

Materials	105
Direct labour	103
Overhead costs	103
	104

The deliveries by the factory to the finished products stores as well as the sales must be costed at current prices (standard costs adjusted by appropriate indices).

There is no work in process at the beginning or at the end of the period. At the end of the period the assets and the shareholders' equity must be revalued on the basis of the following price indices for:

Machinery and equipment	105
Inventories:	
Materials	105
Finished products	104
Shareholders' equity	103

The journal entries of the operations are as follows:

1. *Purchases of materials*

Inventory of materials	$250,000	
Purchase price variances	10,000	
Accounts payable		$260,000

2. *Materials used*

Work in process, materials	235,000	
Inventory of materials		235,000

3. *Direct labour*

Work in process, direct labour	125,000	
Labour rate variances	5,000	
Cash		130,000

4. *Factory overheads*

Work in process, overheads	125,000	
Overhead price level variances	6,000	
Accumulated amortization		5,000
Financial results, interest charge		3,000
Cash		123,000

5. *Deliveries from factory*

Inventory of finished products	480,000	
Finished products price variances (4%)	19,200	
Work in process, materials		240,000
Work in process, direct labour		120,000
Work in process, overheads		120,000
Cost variance absorbed, material (5%)		12,000
Cost variance absorbed, direct labour (3%)		3,600
Cost variance absorbed, overheads (3%)		3,600

6. *Sales*

Accounts receivable	700,000	
Trading account, sales		700,000
Trading account, cost of sales	520,000	
(at standard costs × 1.04)		
Inventory of finished products		500,000
Finished products price variances absorbed		20,000

7. *Selling expenses*

Trading account, cost of sales	$105,000	
Selling expense variance	5,000	
Financial results, interest charge		$4,500
Cash		105,500

8. *Collections and payments*

Cash	650,000	
Accounts receivable		650,000
Accounts payable	300,000	
Financial results, interest on loan	4,000	
Cash		304,000

9. *Transfer of factory variances*

Direct labour variance	5,000	
Overhead costs variance	5,000	
Materials variance		5,000
Work in process account		5,000

After these entries have been posted the following trial balance can be prepared:

Trial Balance at End of Period

	Debit	Credit
Assets		
Machinery and equipment	$ 500,000	
Accumulated amortization		$ 255,000
Inventories:		
Materials	215,000	
Finished products	180,000	
Accounts receivable	320,000	
Cash	367,500	
Liabilities and Equity		
Shareholders' equity		500,000
8% Loan		600,000
Accounts payable		160,000
Trading Results		
Sales		700,000
Cost of sales	520,000	
Selling expenses	105,000	

Price Level Variances

Purchases of materials	$10,000	
Labour rates	5,000	
Overhead costs	6,000	
Finished products	19,200	

Price Level Variances Absorbed

Purchase price variances		$12,000
Labour rate variances		3,600
Overhead cost variances		3,600
Finished products price variances		20,000

Performance and Volume Variances

Factory:

Materials		5,000
Direct labour	5,000	
Overhead costs	5,000	
Selling expenses	5,000	

Financial Results

Interest charges less interest on loan		3,500
Total	**$2,262,700**	**$2,262,700**

The revaluation journal entries at the end of the period are as follows:

10. *Shareholders' equity*

Revaluation adjustments	$ 15,000	
Shareholders' equity		$15,000
(3% of $500,000)		

11. *Fixed assets*

Machinery and equipment	25,000	
(5% of $500,000)		
Accumulated amortization		12,750
(5% of $255,000)		
Revaluation adjustments		12,250
(5% of $245,000)		

12. *Inventory of materials*

Inventory of materials	10,750	
(5% of $215,000)		
Purchase price variances		600
Revaluation adjustments		10,150

13. *Inventory of finished products*

Inventory of finished products (4% of $180,000)	$7,200	
Finished products price variances absorbed	800	
Revaluation adjustments		$8,000

Explanation of Purchase Price Variances

Crediting $600 to the "purchase price variances" needs an explanation. The inventory of materials at standard costs has increased from $200,000 to $215,000. It actually cost 4% more than standard to increase the inventory by $15,000, and therefore the $600 is included in the $10,000 purchase price variance on the total purchases during the period under consideration (See Journal Entry 1). The 5% revaluation of the inventory when applied to the additional stock of $15,000 means an increase by $750, of which $600 was paid for and only $150 was a true revaluation gain.

After this entry has been posted, the purchase price variance account shows a debit balance of $9,400, representing the actual variance on the $235,000 of materials used in manufacturing. Since, according to the assumptions, there is no work in process either at the beginning or at the end of the period, the $9,400 price variance relates to the same quantity that absorbed a price variance of $12,000 (See Journal Entry 5), resulting in a favourable balance of $2,600. The $2,600 consists of two items: $2,350 due to the difference between the actual purchase price level of 104 and the price index of 105 for materials; and $250 related to the favourable material efficiency variance of $5,000. The absorption was based on the standard volume of materials of $240,000 contained in the factory output (See Journal Entry 5), whereas the actual volume of materials was $235,000. Accordingly $250 (5% of $5,000) of the $2,600 is due to the material efficiency variance.

It could be argued that the $250 should be transferred from the group of "price level variances" to the group of "efficiency variances." However, in actual practice one is rarely in a position to make such a complete analysis as in this simplified case study. Fluctuating volumes of work in process complicate matters to such an extent that at some point an analysis must be considered as final. Moreover, it is unlikely that a different conclusion would be drawn if a performance variance is shown as $5,250 instead of $5,000.

Explanation of Finished Products Price Variances

The inventory of finished products decreased during the period in question from $200,000 to $180,000 at standard costs. Of the $20,000 price variances absorbed by sales (See Journal Entry 6), $800 relates to the inventory decrease of $20,000. Since both the index for the factory output and for the costing of sales was the same (104), the absorption account will exactly offset the finished products price variance account after charging it with $800 (4% of $20,000).

After all entries have been posted, the detailed operating results for the period appears as follows:

Operating Results for the Period

			Operating Profit (Loss)
Trading Results			
Sales		$700,000	
Current production cost of sales	$520,000		
Selling expenses at standard	105,000	625,000	
Net trading profit			$75,000
Price Level Variances			
Purchases of materials		2,600	
Labour rates	$ 1,400		
Overhead costs	2,400		
Finished products	—	—	
Net price level variances			($ 1,200)
Performance and Volume Variances			
Materials		$ 5,000	
Direct labour	$ 5,000		
Overhead costs	5,000		
Selling expenses	5,000		
Net performance and volume variances			($10,000)
Financial Results			
Interest on loan	$ 4,000		
Interest charges imputed in costs		$ 7,500	
Residual income			$3,500
Total Operating Profit			$67,300

The revaluation adjustment account appears as follows:

REVALUATION ADJUSTMENT ACCOUNT

Revaluation of equity	$ 15,000	Revaluation of machinery and equipment	$ 12,250
Revaluation surplus	15,400	Revaluation of inventories:	
		Materials	10,150
		Finished products	8,000
	$ 30,400		$ 30,400

The revaluation surplus is mainly due to the favourable monetary position of this company. The liabilities exceed the monetary assets at the beginning of the period by $150,000 and at the end of the period by $72,500, disregarding the profits of the period and assuming that the greater part will be used to pay income taxes and dividends. A small part of the revaluation profit is, in this example, due to the price index for equity (103) being lower than for the physical assets (machinery and equipment 105; materials 105 and finished products 104).

The balance sheet appears as follows:

BALANCE SHEET AT END OF PERIOD

Machinery and equipment	$ 525,000	Equity	$ 515,000
Accumulated amortization	267,750	Revaluation surplus	15,400
Net current value	$ 257,250	Operating profit	67,300
Inventories:		8% Loan	600,000
Materials	$ 225,750	Accounts payable	160,000
Finished products	187,200		
	$ 412,950		
Accounts receivable	$ 320,000		
Cash	367,500		
	$1,357,700		$1,357,700

In this example the standard costs were revised at the end of the period to the current price levels. If that had not been the case, *separate accounts* should have been used to record the increase in value of the inventories, as explained in Section 3.3.

Under the *holding gains concept* the shareholders' equity would remain at $500,000 and the revaluation gain of $30,400 would be included in the revaluation surplus account. If the relative large amount of monetary assets in this example emanated from an amortization or inventory gap, as demonstrated in Chapter 4, the company would be advised to make a provision out of operating profit for the loss of purchasing power on those monetary assets which are committed to the future replacement of fixed assets and inventories. The calculation of the holding gains would then be as follows:

1. Holding gains from the revaluation of assets:
    1.1 Machinery and equipment $12,250
    1.2 Inventories of materials   10,150
    1.3 Inventories of finished products   8,000 $30,400

2. Loss of purchasing power on monetary assets committed to the future replacement of fixed assets and inventories:
    2.1 5% of the accumulated amortization funds
         of $255,000 $12,750
    2.2 4.5% of total inventory reduction of $5,000   225   12,975

Total holding gains required to conserve the
continuity of the enterprise $43,375

6.5 Enterprises with Several Manufacturing Departments

Many manufacturing companies consist of more than one manufacturing department, some of which make certain parts, components or sub-assemblies, while others assemble these or perform certain operations on the parts or the products. The successive processes may be continuous, intermittent or on a job order basis, for one or for a variety of products.

To this type of enterprise the current value concept can be applied in two ways, either

1. By assessing the current value at the *time of sale* in exactly the same way as described in the previous section, or

2. By transferring the "products" of each department at current value to the next department and finally to the sales department

First Method

Under the first method the *entire plant* is considered to be *one operation* for the application of the current value concept. As in Section 6.4, the internal transactions or operations are all recorded at *standard costs* and the differences between actual costs and standard costs are segregated in price variance accounts at the time of purchase of materials and of the payment of labour and overheads. The costs are carried in the work in process accounts at standard. The current value of the sales transactions is calculated at the *time of sale* either by the application of price indices or otherwise, and the differences between standard costs and current values are transferred to one or more "price variance absorption accounts."

This procedure applies to the operations. For the determination of the current value of the fixed assets, inventories of finished products, materials and work in process the same procedure as in the previous section can be followed although the variety of inventories in different stages of completion may cause extra work. On the other hand, with a rate of inflation not exceeding a 5 to 10% level per year, the revaluation of shareholders' equity and assets *continuously* for the purpose of publishing "accurate" monthly or quarterly financial statements does not serve any useful purpose. An *annual revision* of the current value of equity and assets should, in most instances, meet reasonable requirements. However, as explained in the first chapter, it is very important and sometimes essential for the continuity of the enterprise to provide *continuously current values for decision-making purposes,* such as profit control, setting sales policies, pricing of sales, make-or-buy decisions, and capital investment decisions.

Second Method

The entire manufacturing process can be recorded at current values while simultaneously recording the detailed processes at standard costs for the purpose of performance control. In order to do this an additional set of accounts would be opened for *each department* consisting of:

1. *Purchase price variance account*
   to record the price variances on purchases from external suppliers.

2. *Price variance account internal supplies*
   to record the differences between standard costs and current values of goods and services supplied by other departments.

3. *Labour rate variance account*

4. *Overheads variance account*

5. *Price variances absorbed*
   5.1 To record the differences between standard costs and current values of the deliveries to other departments
   5.2 To record the price variances absorbed on the deliveries to finished products stores.

The possibility of recording the entire manufacturing operation on the basis of current values is provided here as a theoretical case only. It requires a great deal of additional work, more risk of clerical errors without apparent additional benefits. For these reasons the first approach is much more preferable.

6.6 Multi-Division Companies

Larger companies may consist of several divisions, each of which is more or less an *integrated enterprise* with its own purchasing, manufacturing and sales to external customers as well as to other divisions of the company. If, within broad overall company policies and on the basis of an approved long range plan, subject to periodic performance reports, full authority is delegated to divisional management with respect to the execution of the approved plans, the divisions operate as *profit centres*, with the performance of a division being judged by its *rate of return* on the capital funds invested in that division.

Profit Centre Concept

For a successful application of the profit centre concept the company's top management must permit the divisions to compete. The profit centres must be free to trade with outsiders as well as with other divisions, whichever is to the best advantage of the particular division involved. The importance of this is emphasized by Breech:[2]

> Under the profit center system, revenue control of intercompany sales between various divisions of the same firm gives invaluable guidance in make-or-buy decisions, provides a check on supplier prices, and is a useful test of performance. Moreover, requiring our own producing divisions to sell competitively to the end-products divisions (car, truck and tractor divisions) has contributed enormously to the improved profit position of Ford Motor Company.

and by Dean[3]:

> The modern integrated, multi-product firm functions best if it is made into a sort of miniature of the competitive, free-enterprise system. The firm should be comprised of independent operating units that act like economic entitites, free to trade outside the company as well as inside. Each such entity or profit centre will, in seeking to maximize its own profit, do what will maximize the profits of the entire company, just as individual firms in a private enterprise society, by seeking their selfish advancement, generate the high productivity and well-being of a competitive economy.

Profit Centre Procedure

The current value concept can be applied to each division, each with its own accounting system, its own balance sheet and income statement. The "shareholders' equity" of a division is represented by its *intercompany control account* with the head office. Monetary assets and liabilities may include trading accounts with other divisions and should be treated as regular accounts receivable and accounts payable. In the consolidation of the financial statements, the intercompany accounts (control and trade accounts) will be eliminated in the usual manner, producing a consolidated balance sheet in which equity as well as assets are valued on the basis of current values.

The consolidated profit will be the aggregate of the divisional profits with the exception of the revaluation adjustments. Each division will show either a deficit or a surplus adjustment, depending on the price level changes during the period under consideration and the structure of the balance sheet at the end of the period. The summary of the divisional adjustments should be combined with the adjustments of the intercompany accounts with the divisions in the books of head office. It is evident that an increase of a division's "equity" creates an equal revaluation gain in head office, which must be combined with the adjustments in the books of the divisions to obtain a complete picture of the concern's revaluation. The example at the end of this section illustrates this point.

Transfer Prices

The fact that transfers between profit centres are made on the basis of market prices, if available and applicable, does in no way interfere with the current value concept. To the contrary, a transfer price based on market conditions and mutually agreed to by both parties concerned is the best possible interpretation of current value.

This applies even to cases in which a transfer price is based on the *direct costs* of the supplying division in a period that the facilities of the supplying division are underloaded and divisional management attempts to obtain additional sales at differential prices, either on the external or on the internal market. The current value in cases like this is equal to the transfer price representing the best attainable price and relevant to the valuation of the inventories of the receiving division.

An example of a company with two divisions (or subsidiaries), the balance sheets of which appear as follows before the revaluation, illustrates the procedure of revaluation and consolidation:

Balance Sheets at End of Period before Revaluation

	Division A	Division B	Head Office	Consolidated
Assets				
Fixed assets	$500,000	$ 500,000	$ 300,000	$1,300,000
Accumulated amortization	400,000	100,000	100,000	600,000
Net fixed assets	$100,000	$ 400,000	$ 200,000	$ 700,000

Inventories	$200,000	$ 350,000	$ —	$ 550,000
Accounts receivable:				
External	100,000	150,000	—	250,000
Internal	50,000	60,000	—	—
Divisional control account	—	—	1,050,000	—
Cash	100,000	100,000	150,000	350,000
	$550,000	$1,060,000	$1,400,000	$1,850,000

Shareholders' Equity and Liabilities				
Shareholders' equity	$ —	$ —	$1,300,000	$1,300,000
Head office control acct.	300,000	750,000	—	—
Accounts payable:				
External	150,000	200,000	100,000	450,000
Internal	60,000	50,000	—	—
Operating profit	40,000	60,000	—	100,000
	$550,000	$1,060,000	$1,400,000	$1,850,000

The revaluation is done on the basis of the following indices for:

	Division A	Division B	Head Office
Fixed assets	110	108	105
Inventories	105	106	—
Shareholders' equity	106	106	106

After revaluation on the basis of the above indices, the balance sheets appear as follows:

Balance Sheets at End of Period after Revaluation

	Division A	Division B	Head Office	Consolidated
Assets				
Fixed assets	$550,000	$ 540,000	$ 315,000	$1,405,000
Accumulated amortization	440,000	108,000	105,000	653,000
Net fixed assets	$110,000	$ 432,000	$ 210,000	$ 752,000
Inventories	210,000	371,000	—	581,000
Accounts receivable:				
External	100,000	150,000	—	250,000
Internal	50,000	60,000	—	—
Division control account	—	—	1,113,000	—
Cash	100,000	100,000	150,000	350,000
	$570,000	$1,113,000	$1,473,000	$1,933,000

Shareholders' Equity and Liabilities				
Shareholders' equity	$ —	$ —	$1,378,000	$1,378,000
Head Office control acct.	318,000	795,000	—	—
Accounts payable:				
External	150,000	200,000	100,000	450,000
Internal	60,000	50,000	—	—
Operating profit	40,000	60,000	—	100,000
Revaluation surplus	2,000	8,000	(5,000)	5,000
	$570,000	$1,113,000	$1,473,000	$1,933,000

Under the *holding gains concept* two solutions are possible; in the first solution the holding gains emanating from the revaluation of the assets could be increased, as was done in Section 6.4, by a provision to offset the loss of purchasing power of that part of the monetary assets which was derived from the accumulated amortization of fixed assets. In this case the holding gains would be as follows from:

1. Revaluation of the assets $83,000

2. Loss of purchasing power of the amortization,
   converted into monetary assets   53,000

   Total $136,000

The $53,000 loss on the amortization gap reduces, in this case, the total operating profit to $47,000.

For the other solution it can be argued as in Section 5.5 that, although the divisions individually might have an amortization gap, this is to all appearances probably not so for the company as a whole. The final answer to this depends on two points, namely:

1. The extent to which the assets are distributed with respect to age,

2. The extent to which new investments and amortization match.

As was demonstrated in Section 5.5, as soon as the age distribution of the fixed assets approach the "ideal complex" situation, new investments can be entirely financed by the released amortization funds, in which case the "amortization gap" ceases to exist. As long as this ideal situation has not been achieved, an estimate should be made of the size of the amortization gap.

6.7 Overhead Costs and Current Values

Difficulty of Segregating Price Level Changes

It may be difficult to isolate price level changes from the overhead costs during the period between revisions of standard costs and expense budgets, assuming that the type of standard cost system in use is based on the latest costs at the time of revision.

Whereas the segregation of the differences between standard and actual purchase prices of material as well as between standard and actual labour rates is mainly a *routine procedure*, once the standard cost prices and standard labour rates have been set, the segregation of the variances from other cost classifications requires considerable work. Every item would have to be verified, at the time of payment, with the price or rate level upon which the cost standards or cost budgets were based. This is not only time consuming due to the variety and the large number of items, but more so because in larger companies the procedure followed to authorize payment of these costs does not lend itself to segregation of the variances at the same time. Moreover, variances from the standard price or rate level are not always easy to recognize as such. For instance, with the remuneration of management and supervisory staff, travel and entertainment expenses, a reduction in the number of employees in a department may be achieved by paying higher salaries for fewer but more highly skilled employees, resulting in lower overall costs.

As long as the rate of inflation or price level changes stay within manageable limits (say 5% per year), it usually is a more efficient procedure to charge the *actual* overhead costs to the operations. This procedure is not recommended for the costs of direct material, productive labour and other direct and easily measureable costs. In the first place, as mentioned before, the segregation of price variances from these costs is not a problem as it is with overhead costs. In the second place, the control of direct costs is of a quantitative nature based on a comparison of actual quantities (of material and time) with standard quantities, both valued at standard prices and rates. The level of these prices and rates is irrelevant for performance control within rather wide limits.

Another advantage of charging the overhead costs at actual to the operations is that it keeps departmental and higher management continuously informed of the price level changes in the overhead costs. This may have an effect on departmental policies with respect to the structure of the overhead costs. For example, sharp increases in certain cost items, such as in salaries, may justify the purchase of more or better equipment in order to offset higher salary costs.

Alternative Procedure

On the other hand, a departmental manager cannot be held *responsible* for the price level changes after his cost budget is established. Since it is much easier to assess the effect of price level changes by *department*, after the costs have been allocated to the departments involved, than at the time of payment by *cost classifications*, two solutions present themselves.

1. Eliminate the effect of the price level changes from the actual departmental costs, or

2. Adjust the cost standards or cost budgets by a cost index to offset the effect of the price level changes.

The amount of the adjustment in either case should be transferred to an "overhead price level variance account." This is the same account as mentioned in Section 6.4.

The second approach seems to be the most appropriate. It does not save any work, for in order to be able to calculate the cost index the difference between the actual and the standard cost level must be estimated or calculated first. Yet with the second method there is the advantage that the cost accounts show the actual costs which may be useful for later analyses.

6.8 Service Industries and Current Values

Everything that has been said in the previous sections of this chapter on manufacturing can equally be applied to service industries. The application of the current value concept in these enterprises is easier, since no material costs or material inventories of significance are involved. However, materials for repair and maintenance, replacement of worn out parts in equipment, auxiliary materials and the like, can be treated in the same manner as in manufacturing enterprises.

The rates which these enterprises charge for their services are then based on standard rates adjusted individually or by a price index to reflect the current value of the services rendered. The same procedure can be followed for the internal services of a company, such as those provided by a maintenance or transportation department, with the difference that internal services would be charged at cost to the department using these services, unless the internal service department is organized as a profit centre.

Notes

1. R. I. Dickey, "Setting Standard Costs," in *Cost Accountants' Handbook*. New York: The Ronald Press, 1960.
2. E. R. Breech, "How did Ford do it?" in *The Journal of Accountancy* (February, 1956).
3. In *Harvard Business Review*, vol. 33.

Chapter 7

INTEGRATION OF MANAGEMENT AND CUSTODIAL ACCOUNTING IN ONE ACCOUNTING SYSTEM

7.1 Introduction

The accounting system can be organized in such a way that the accounts contain the information for managerial purposes as well as for income tax or other custodial purposes. This can be done in two ways, depending on which objective is deemed to be the more important of the two. If *custodial accounting* is considered to be of prime importance, then the accounting system and in particular the chart of accounts should be designed in such a way that the accounts for assets and liabilities as well as for revenue and expenditures produce the custodial financial statements. To this a number of accounts are added, first for the adjustments to the valuation of the assets and second to break down revenue and expenditures in such a manner that the requirements of management can be met.

The other method is exactly the opposite. First the accounts are designed to meet the managerial requirements, to which are then added a number of accounts for the adjustments to the valuation of the assets and for the income accounting under the custodial concept.

Since accounting for management should have priority, in the author's opinion, the second approach is preferable. Moreover, the second method is technically simpler due to the fact that the number of additional accounts needed to meet the custodial requirements is considerably smaller than under the first method. For custodial accounting, the breakdown of income and expenses is very limited as compared with that required for managerial purposes.

In the following section examples are used to demonstrate how the "custodial" balance sheet and income statement are derived from the "managerial" statements and accounts, followed by a section in which it is demonstrated how both types of statements are produced by *one* system of accounts.

7.2 System Designed Primarily for Management Accounting

The derivation of the custodial accounts from the managerial accounts may be best explained by an example. The "managerial" balance sheet as at January 1, 1973 is as follows:

BALANCE SHEET AS AT JANUARY 1, 1973

Fixed assets	$1,500,000	Equity (Capital stock plus reserves)	$1,820,000
Accumulated amortization of fixed assets	750,000	Deferred income taxes	180,000
Net current value	$ 750,000	Income taxes payable 1972	50,000
Inventories	1,200,000	Dividend payable 1972	50,000
Accounts receivable	1,000,000	Accounts payable	1,000,000
Cash	150,000		
	$3,100,000		$3,100,000

The valuation for managerial purposes is based on *current values* (under the equity concept), the valuation for income tax purposes on *historical costs.*

The balance sheet prepared for income tax purposes is as follows:

BALANCE SHEET AS AT JANUARY 1, 1973

Fixed assets	$1,000,000	Equity	$1,550,000
Accumulated amortization of fixed assets	500,000	Income taxes payable 1972	50,000
		Dividend payable 1972	50,000
Net book value	$ 500,000	Accounts payable	1,000,000
Inventories	1,000,000		
Accounts receivable	1,000,000		
Cash	150,000		
	$2,650,000		$2,650,000

The following transactions took place during 1973:

1. Purchases:

Merchandise	$2,100,000
Fixed assets	150,000

2. Sales — $3,000,000

3. Cost of sales, at historical costs — $2,000,000
   at current values — 2,100,000

4. Amortization of fixed assets:

10% of purchase price at current value	$ 150,000
Capital cost allowance:	
Standard allowance 20% of book value as at year end	130,000
Extra allowance 10% of book value	65,000
Total capital cost allowance	195,000

5. Other costs, paid for by cash $ 500,000

6. Payments:
   Income tax 1972 $ 50,000
   Dividend 1972   50,000
   Accounts payable   2,250,000

7. Collected on accounts receivable $3,000,000

8. At year end the fixed assets, excluding the addition of $150,000 which was bought in December 1973, the inventories and the shareholders' equity are to be revalued upwards, all by 10%.

9. Income taxes are 40% of taxable income.

After the entries for the transactions 1 to 7 have been posted, the trial balance appears as follows:

Trial Balance as at December 31, 1973

	Debit	Credit
Fixed assets	$1,650,000	—
Accumulated amortization of fixed assets	—	$ 900,000
Inventories	1,200,000	—
Accounts receivable	1,000,000	—
Cash	300,000	—
Shareholders' equity	—	1,820,000
Deferred income taxes	—	180,000
Accounts payable	—	1,000,000
Sales	—	3,000,000
Cost of sales	2,100,000	—
Amortization of fixed assets	150,000	—
Other costs	500,000	—
	$6,900,000	$6,900,000

The journal entries for the revaluation of assets and shareholders' equity, item 8, are as follows:

Revaluation adjustments	$182,000	
Shareholders' equity		$182,000
(10% of $1,820,000)		
Fixed assets	150,000	
(10% of $1,500,000)		
Accumulated amortization of fixed assets		90,000
(10% of $900,000)		
Revaluation adjustments		60,000

Inventories		$120,000
(10% of $1,200,000)		
Revaluation adjustments		$120,000

After these entries the revaluation adjustment account shows a loss of $2,000 which is charged to the "managerial" income account. This account, after the income taxes have been calculated, would then appear as follows:

PROFIT AND LOSS ACCOUNT 1973

Cost of sales	$2,100,000	Sales	$3,000,000
Amortization of fixed assets	150,000		
Other costs	500,000		
Gross profit	250,000		
			$3,000,000
	$3,000,000		
Income taxes:		Gross profit	$ 250,000
Normal 40% of $250,000	$ 100,000		
40% tax on revaluation of assets	72,000		
Revaluation loss	2,000		
Net profit, available			
for distribution	76,000		
	$ 250,000		$ 250,000

Latent Income Tax Obligations

The increase in the value of the assets by $180,000 ($60,000 for fixed assets and $120,000 for inventories) creates a *latent tax obligation* of $72,000. The higher asset values will in due course induce *higher charges* (amortization and cost of sales) to the income account, but because the income tax calculation is based on historical costs, the higher charges will *be added back to income* in future years. This happened in 1973 with respect to the cost of sales, $100,000 of which is added back to income.

    A further analysis may clarify this point, particularly the reconciliation of the increase in the latent tax liability at the end of 1973 by $72,000 charged to the profit and loss account. First the calculation of the *increase in the latent tax liability*, which at year end amounts to 40% of the *difference in asset valuations*:

Current value of the assets (after the revaluation at year end):

1.	Fixed assets ($1,800,000 − $990,000)	$ 810,000
2.	Inventories	1,320,000
3.	Total current value	$2,130,000

Historical cost of the assets:

1. Fixed assets:

Book value as at January 1, 1973	$ 500,000	
Purchases	150,000	
	$ 650,000	
Capital cost allowance 1973	195,000	
Book value as at December 31, 1973	$ 455,000	
2. Inventories as at December 31, 1973	1,100,000	
3. Total book value at historical cost		1,555,000
Latent taxable income		$ 575,000

40% of which amounts to a latent tax liability at the year end of $230,000
The latent tax liability as at January 1, 1973 amounted to 40%
of the difference between the asset valuations as at that date
which was $450,000 ($1,950,000 − $1,500,000)   180,000

Additional provision required at year end $ 50,000

This may be reconciled with the charge of $72,000 to the profit
and loss account as follows:

1. 40% of the revaluation of the assets
   by $180,000 at the year end $ 72,000

2. Less 40% of the difference between
   income based on current values and
   taxable income, consisting of:

2.1 Lower cost of sales	$100,000	
2.2 Higher amortization of fixed assets	45,000	
Higher taxable income	$ 55,000	
40% of which amounts to		22,000

3. Balance to be added to latent tax liability $ 50,000

One could also say that the sum of $22,000 relates to previous years and
should be charged to the provision for latent tax liabilities. This account
would then appear as follows:

DEFERRED INCOME TAXES 1973

Dec. 31 Income tax payable related to prior years	$ 22,000	Jan. 1 Opening balance	$180,000
Dec. 31 Closing balance	230,000	Dec. 31 Charged to profit and loss 40% of asset revaluaton	72,000
	$252,000		$252,000

Statements for Income Tax Purposes

The usual procedure to establish taxable income starts with the income as calculated by the company, in our example the income based on current values, before deducting provisions for income taxes and revaluation adjustments, thus as follows:

Profit as per financial statements	$250,000
Add: Difference in cost of sales	100,000
	$350,000
Less: Difference in amortization	45,000
Taxable income	$305,000
Income taxes payable at 40%	$122,000

In actual practice, the number of additions and deductions may be much greater, but the procedure is the same.

The other method of *comparing equities*, based on historical costs, has the same result:

1. Shareholders' equity at the year end:

Fixed assets	$ 455,000	
Inventories	1,100,000	
Accounts receivable	1,000,000	
Cash	300,000	
Total assets		$2,855,000
Less: Accounts payable		1,000,000
		$1,855,000

2. Shareholders' equity at the previous year end — 1,550,000

3. Taxable income — $ 305,000

The "managerial" balance sheet at the year end now appears as follows:

BALANCE SHEET AS AT DECEMBER 31, 1973

Fixed assets	$1,800,000	Equity	$2,002,000
Accumulated amortization of fixed assets	990,000	Deferred income taxes	230,000
		Net profit, after income taxes	76,000
Net current value	$ 810,000	Income taxes payable 1973	122,000
Inventories	1,320,000	Accounts payable	1,000,000
Accounts receivable	1,000,000		
Cash	300,000		
	$3,430,000		$3,430,000

The "custodial" balance sheet, based on historical cost, would appear as follows:

BALANCE SHEET AS AT DECEMBER 31, 1973

Fixed assets	$1,150,000	Equity *	$1,550,000
Capital cost allowances	695,000	Net profit, after income taxes	183,000
Net book value	$ 455,000	Income taxes payable 1973	122,000
Inventories	1,100,000	Accounts payable	1,000,000
Accounts receivable	1,000,000		
Cash	300,000		
	$2,855,000		$2,855,000

*Gross shareholders' equity as calculated on the previous page		$1,855,000
Less: Income taxes payable for 1973	$122,000	
Net profit for 1973	183,000	305,000
Shareholders' equity at the year end		$1,550,000

The profit and loss account, also based on historical cost, is:

PROFIT AND LOSS ACCOUNT 1973

Cost of sales	$2,000,000	Sales	$3,000,000
Amortization of fixed assets	195,000		
Other costs	500,000		
Income tax payable	122,000		
Net profit, after income taxes	183,000		
	$3,000,000		$3,000,000

Financial Statements for Other Purposes

So far we have assumed that the "custodial" financial statements are identical with those prepared for the shareholders, securities commissions, tax authorities and other government agencies, but this is not necessarily so. The statements prepared for income tax purposes and those based on current values represent probably the two *extremes in a spectrum* of possibilities. The first are governed by income tax laws; the latter by a set of accounting principles based on economic science.

What is presented to the shareholders and the public may be subject to other considerations than those prepared for managerial purposes. If one believes that historical costs or a variant to historical costs, such as LIFO, are better suited for presentation than current values or that inventories should be valued at *direct costs*, or at *full costs* but without the imputed interest charges, there is no law against it. Without a set of principles, but only a set of conventions or rules to provide a certain degree of consistency, the variety of possibilities in statement preparation and presentation is unlimited!

7.3   Integrated System of Accounts

As mentioned in Section 7.1 the *integration* of management and custodial accounts consists of two sets of accounts:

1. A set of accounts for managerial purposes only, and

2. Another set of adjustment accounts for the differences between managerial (current) values and custodial (historical) values,

in such a way that the combination of the two sets produces the custodial financial balance sheet and income account. In this process it is not necessary to provide for a breakdown of the custodial income. What may be required in this respect, such as total sales and total costs, can easily be derived from the management accounting section.

Using the same example as in the previous section, the general ledger accounts are opened with a journal entry based on the following trial balance:

Trial Balance as at January 1, 1973 ($000's omitted)

	Management Accounts		Adjustment Accounts		Custodial Accounts	
	Debit	Credit	Debit	Credit	Debit	Credit
Fixed assets	$1,500	$ —	$—	$500	$1,000	$ —
Accumulated amortization of fixed assets	—	750	250	—	—	500
Inventories	1,200	—	—	200	1,000	—

Accounts receivable	1,000	—	—	—	1,000	—
Cash	150	—	—	—	150	—
Shareholders' equity	—	1,820	270	—	—	1,550
Deferred income taxes	—	180	180	—	—	—
Income tax payable 1972	—	50	—	—	—	50
Dividend payable 1972	—	50	—	—	—	50
Accounts payable	—	1,000	—	—	—	1,000
Totals	$3,850	$3,850	$700	$700	$3,150	$3,150

The journal entry is as follows:

Fixed assets	$1,500,000	
Inventories	1,200,000	
Accounts receivable	1,000,000	
Cash	150,000	
Accumulated amortization of fixed assets		$ 750,000
Shareholders' equity		1,820,000
Deferred income taxes		180,000
Income taxes payable 1972		50,000
Dividend payable 1972		50,000
Accounts payable		1,000,000

and for the differences between the two accounting objectives:

Adjustment of accumulated amortization of fixed assets	$ 250,000	
Adjustment of shareholders' equity	270,000	
Adjustment of deferred income taxes	180,000	
Adjustment of fixed assets		$ 500,000
Adjustment of inventories		200,000

From the various transactions given in the previous section, the following collective journal entries are to be made, using the same accounts as mentioned above:

1. *Purchases*

Inventories	$2,100,000	
Fixed assets	150,000	
Accounts payable		$2,250,000

2. *Sales*

Accounts receivable	3,000,000	
Sales		3,000,000

3. *Cost of sales*

Cost of sales, at current values	2,100,000	
Inventories		2,100,000

Adjustment of inventories	$ 100,000	
Adjustment of profit and loss account		$ 100,000

Note

If the cost of sales at historical cost is continuously available, the entry for the difference between the cost of sales at current prices and at historical cost could be made periodically. However, the cost of sales on the basis of historical cost, in an accounting system designed for management purposes, would normally be available only with considerable extra work. It is much easier to make one entry at year end after the historical cost of the closing inventory has been determined, on the basis of which the cost of sales can be found as follows:

Opening inventory, at historical cost	$1,000,000
Purchases in 1973	2,100,000
	$3,100,000
Closing inventory, at historical cost	1,100,000
Cost of sales	$2,000,000

This is $100,000 less than the current value of the cost of sales, necessitating the above entry in the custodial section of the accounts.

4. *Amortization of fixed assets*

Cost of amortization of fixed assets	$ 150,000	
Accumulated amortization of fixed assets		$ 150,000
Adjustment of profit and loss account	45,000	
Adjustment of accumulated amortization of fixed assets (for the diference with the higher capital cost allowance)		45,000

5. *Other costs*

Other costs	500,000	
Cash		500,000

6. *Payments*

Accounts payable	2,250,000	
Dividend payable 1972	50,000	
Income tax payable 1972	50,000	
Cash		2,350,000

7. *Collections*

Cash	$3,000,000	
Accounts receivable		$3,000,000

8. *Revaluation of assets and shareholders' equity*

Revaluation adjustments	182,000	
Shareholders' equity		182,000
Fixed assets	150,000	
Accumulated amortization of fixed assets		90,000
Revaluation adjustments		60,000
Inventories	120,000	
Revaluation adjustments		120,000
Profit and loss account	2,000	
Revaluation adjustments		2,000
(to close off to profit and loss)		

and to offset the revaluation for custodial purposes:

Adjustment of shareholders' equity	182,000	
Adjustment of accumulated amortization of fixed assets	90,000	
Adjustment of fixed assets		150,000
Adjustment of inventories		120,000
Adjustment of profit and loss account		2,000

9. *Closing off the revenue and cost accounts at year end*

Sales	$3,000,000	
Cost of sales		$2,100,000
Cost of amortization fixed assets		150,000
Other costs		500,000
Profit and loss account		250,000
(for the gross profit)		
Profit and loss account	172,000	
Income tax payable 1973		122,000
Deferred income taxes		50,000

and in the section of the custodial adjustment accounts:

Adjustment of deferred income taxes	50,000	
Adjustment of profit and loss account		50,000

After posting these entries, the general ledger accounts for 1973 appear as follows:

1. Managerial Accounts

FIXED ASSETS

Jan. 1	Opening balance	$1,500,000	Dec. 31 Closing balance	$1,800,000
1973	Purchases	150,000		
Dec. 31	Revaluation adjustment	150,000		
		$1,800,000		$1,800,000

ACCUMULATED AMORTIZATION OF FIXED ASSETS

Dec. 31 Closing balance		$990,000	Jan. 1 Opening balance	$750,000
			1973 Amortization	150,000
			Dec. 31 Revaluation adjustment	90,000
		$990,000		$990,000

INVENTORIES

Jan. 1	Opening balance	$1,200,000	1973 Cost of sales	$2,100,000
1973	Purchases	2,100,000	Dec. 31 Closing balance	1,320,000
Dec. 31	Revaluation adjustment	120,000		
		$3,420,000		$3,420,000

ACCOUNTS RECEIVABLE

Jan. 1	Opening balance	$1,000,000	1973 Collections	$3,000,000
1973	Sales	3,000,000	Dec. 31 Closing balance	1,000,000
		$4,000,000		$4,000,000

CASH

Jan. 1	Opening balance	$ 150,000	1973 Other costs	$ 500,000
1973	Collections	3,000,000	1973 Payments	2,350,000
			Dec. 31 Closing balance	300,000
		$3,150,000		$3,150,000

SHAREHOLDERS' EQUITY

Dec. 31 Closing balance		$2,002,000	Jan. 1 Opening balance	$1,820,000
			Dec. 31 Revaluation	182,000
		$2,002,000		$2,002,000

DEFERRED INCOME TAXES

Dec. 31 Closing balance	$230,000	Jan. 1 Opening balance	$180,000
		Dec. 31 Transferred to profit and loss account	50,000
	$230,000		$230,000

INCOME TAX PAYABLE 1972

1973 Paid	$ 50,000	Jan. 1 Opening balance	$ 50,000
	$ 50,000		$ 50,000

DIVIDEND PAYABLE 1972

1973 Paid	$ 50,000	Jan. 1 Opening balance	$ 50,000
	$ 50,000		$ 50,000

ACCOUNTS PAYABLE

1973 Payments	$2,250,000	Jan. 1 Opening balance	$1,000,000
Dec. 31 Closing balance	1,000,000	1973 Purchases	2,250,000
	$3,250,000		$3,250,000

INCOME TAX PAYABLE 1973

Dec. 31 Closing balance	$ 122,000	Dec. 31 Transferred to profit and loss account	$ 122,000
	$ 122,000		$ 122,000

SALES

Dec. 31 Transferred to profit and loss account	$3,000,000	1973 Sales	$3,000,000
	$3,000,000		$3,000,000

COST OF SALES

1973 Current cost of sales	$2,100,000	Dec. 31 Transferred to profit and loss account	$2,100,000
	$2,100,000		$2,100,000

COST OF AMORTIZATION OF FIXED ASSETS

1973 10% of current value at beginning of year	$ 150,000	Dec. 31 Transferred to profit and loss account	$ 150,000
	$ 150,000		$ 150,000

OTHER COSTS

1973 Payments	$ 500,000	Dec. 31 Transferred to profit and loss account	$ 500,000
	$ 500,000		$ 500,000

REVALUATION ADJUSTMENTS

Dec. 31 Revaluation of equity	$ 182,000	Dec. 31 Revaluation fo fixed assets	$ 60,000
		Dec. 31 Revaluation of inventories	120,000
		Dec. 31 Loss transferred to profit and loss account	2,000
	$ 182,000		$ 182,000

PROFIT AND LOSS

Dec. 31 Revaluation loss	$ 2,000	Dec. 31 Gross profit	$ 250,000
Dec. 31 Income taxes liability	172,000		
Dec. 31 Net profit	76,000		
	$ 250,000		$ 250,000

2. Custodial Adjustment Accounts

ADJUSTMENT OF FIXED ASSETS

Dec. 31 Cosing balance	$ 650,000	Jan. 1 Opening balance	$ 500,000
		Dec. 31 Adjustment of the revaluation	150,000
	$ 650,000		$ 650,000

ADJUSTMENT OF ACCUMULATED AMORTIZATION OF FIXED ASSETS

Jan. 1 Opening balance	$ 250,000	1973 Additional amortization for 1973	$ 45,000
Dec. 31 Adjustment of the revaluation	90,000	Dec. 31 Closing balance	295,000
	$ 340,000		$ 340,000

ADJUSTMENT OF INVENTORIES

Dec. 31 Adjustment of the cost of sales	$ 100,000	Jan. 1 Opening balance	$ 200,000
Dec. 31 Closing balance	220,000	Dec. 31 Adjustment of the revaluation	120,000
	$ 320,000		$ 320,000

ADJUSTMENT OF SHAREHOLDERS' EQUITY

Jan. 1 Opening balance	$ 270,000	Dec. 31 Closing balance		$ 452,000
Dec. 31 Adjustment of the revaluation	182,000			
	$ 452,000			$ 452,000

ADJUSTMENT OF DEFERRED INCOME TAXES

Jan. 1 Opening balance	$ 180,000	Dec. 31 Closing balance	$ 230,000
Dec. 31 Adjustment of the revaluation	50,000		
	$ 230,000		$ 230,000

ADJUSTMENT OF PROFIT AND LOSS

1973 Additional amortization of fixed assets	$ 45,000	Dec. 31 Revaluation loss	$ 2,000
Dec. 31. Balance of the adjustments	107,000	Dec. 31 Adjustments of cost of sales	100,000
		Dec. 31 Deferred income taxes liability	50,000
	$ 152,000		$ 152,000

After all entries have been posted, the following trial balance at year end can be prepared, in which the accounts of the management section of the chart of accounts and the custodial adjustment accounts have been placed side by side. The two sets of columns combined produce the custodial balance sheet.

Trial Balance as at December 31, 1973 ($000's omitted)

	Management Accounts		Adjustment Accounts		Custodial Accounts	
	Debit	Credit	Debit	Credit	Debit	Credit
Fixed assets	$1,800	$ —	$—	$650	$1,150	$ —
Accumulated amortization of fixed assets	—	990	295	—	—	695
Inventories	1,320	—	—	220	1,100	—
Accounts receivable	1,000	—	—	—	1,000	—
Cash	300	—	—	—	300	
Shareholders' equity	—	2,002	452	—	—	1,550
Deferred income taxes	—	230	230	—	—	—
Income taxes payable 1973	—	122	—	—	—	122
Accounts payable	—	1,000	—	—	—	1,000
Net profit, after income taxes	—	76	—	107	—	183
Totals	$4,420	$4,420	$977	$977	$3,550	$3,550

In actual practice a great many more accounts, mainly in the management section, will be required, in particular the sections in which revenues and costs are recorded, but the technique would be identical to this illustration regardless of the number of accounts and the size of the company.

Quarterly Statements

It was assumed in the examples of this and the previous sections that the custodial statements would be required only once per year. This is the case for income tax purposes, but for other purposes, such as reports for shareholders, *quarterly reports* may be required, in which case the adjustments would have to be calculated and recorded quarterly.

As a final point to this paragraph we assume that $50,000 of the net profit of $76,000 will be paid out to the shareholders, whereas the balance will be set aside as a reserve; this leads to the following entry in the books:

Profit and loss account	$ 76,000	
Dividend payable 1973		$ 50,000
Shareholders' equity		26,000
(retained earnings)		

and in the custodial accounts section:

Adjustment of profit and loss account	107,000	
Adjustment of shareholders' equity		107,000
(retained earnings)		

7.4   System of Accounts For More Than Two Purposes

It is conceivable, as noted in the last part of Section 7.2, that management may want to present the shareholders with a financial report that is different from the information required for internal (managerial) purposes and also different from the information prepared for income tax purposes.

Without entering into a discussion of the motivation of management for this policy — this may be different from company to company — management may prefer to show a financial picture of the company based on historical costs, but in variance with the picture for income tax purposes. This presentation may include a provision for latent income tax liabilities or for other contingent liabilities, such as provisions for warranties, for bad debts, for obsolete inventories and such, which may appear in the managerial accounts but are not acceptable for income tax purposes.

To set up a chart of accounts that would provide for three or more purposes becomes too complicated. It is far more practical to design a chart of accounts which provides for two of the most important purposes and to derive the information for the third purpose from the accounts and from additional notes and calculations.

Chapter 8

SPECIAL CASES

8.1 Technological Price Decreases

It is a common phenomenon that the costs and prices of many products, in particular mass-produced industrial products, rise less than the general price level as indicated by the Consumer Price Index or the GNE Implicit Price Index. This is due to technological changes in product design or formulae and to changes in production methods, as a result of which the unit cost of a product may drop appreciably in a rather short time. Although a substantial decline in unit cost is an exception, the general trend is towards the costs and the prices of mass-produced industrial products rising more slowly than the general price level. With a stable price level, or in a situation without inflation, prices of industrial products would indeed show a decreasing trend. However, in times of inflation this phenomenon is obscured to some extent by the inflationary forces.

The consequences of this phenomenon have a peculiar effect upon the income of an enterprise. Under the historical cost concept, the consequences would be buried in the cost of sales and not emerge separately. But under the current value concept of accounting the effects on income can be readily shown, thereby providing management with valuable information for policy making and planning.

A company engaged in manufacturing industrial products subject to the above-mentioned, relative technological price decreases experiences continuous losses due to the fact that the loss of purchasing power of the shareholders' equity is only partly absorbed by the rising value of the inventories. An example will illustrate this situation.

Assume that in the example used in Section 2.2, the current purchase price at year end is $10.70 per unit as compared to $10.00 at the beginning of the year. With a general inflation rate of 10% per year, and under the *equity concept* based on the *general inflation rate* the revaluation adjustment account would have appeared as follows:

REVALUATION ADJUSTMENT ACCOUNT 1973

Dec. 31 Revaulation of equity by 10%	$ 10,000	Dec. 31 Revaluation of inventory by 7%	$ 7,000
		Dec. 31 Loss	3,000
	$ 10,000		$ 10,000

and the balance sheet at the year end would have been:

BALANCE SHEET AS AT DECEMBER 31, 1973

Inventory	$107,000	Equity:	
Cash	5,000	Original	$100,000
		Adjustment	10,000
		Current value	$110,000
		Operating profit	$5,000
		Revaluation loss	3,000
		Profit	2,000
	$112,000		$112,000

Allowance in Costs

If losses due to technological price decreases occur regularly, are unavoidable and thus inherent to the type of business, these should be considered as *a normal cost* and be included in the product unit costs. They would become part of the operational results. Having been made aware of these costs, management should then try to recover them by raising the selling prices or if the market does not permit this, by taking these costs into consideration in formulating sales policies and in planning. These costs should also be taken into account in calculating the most economical lot sizes (in manufacturing and purchasing) and the most economical inventory level, since it is evident that lower inventories result in lower losses due to technological price decreases.

Equity Based on General Purchasing Power

The *general purchasing power equity concept* is based on the view that it is management's responsibility both to *conserve shareholders' equity* and to *keep shareholders' income inflation-proof*. This policy creates surplus cash in the company because the original business volume (of 10,000 items in the example of Section 2.2) requires less funds (only $107,000) to carry it into the next year. After paying out the entire net profit of $2,000 an amount of $3,000 cash is surplus.

Management may use this surplus to finance a natural growth or an expansion of the company, measured in quantities of course, or to diversify into different activities. "Expansion" may well be a necessity in order to conserve the purchasing power of the shareholders' income. Without this type of growth to offset the effects of the continuous technological price decreases of industrial products, the company's *dollar volume of business would continuously shrink*.

Equity Based on Specific Purchasing Power

The *specific purchasing power equity concept* under which the equity is adjusted on the basis of the specific rate of inflation as evidenced by the price level rise of the individual assets of the company involved, does *not* recognize technological price decreases as a loss. In this case the balance sheet at year end would appear as follows:

BALANCE SHEET AS AT DECEMBER 31, 1973

Inventory	$107,000	Equity:	
		Original	$100,000
		Adjustment 7%	7,000
Cash	5,000	Current value	$107,000
		Profit	5,000
	$112,000		$112,000

Under this concept, after the profit of $5,000 is paid out the company is left with adequate funds to continue the business on the basis of the *same volume* (in quantity) as before.

It is evident that the effects of this concept are:

1. A continuously shrinking dollar volume of business, but

2. For the participants in the revenues and profit, which include the shareholders, management and staff, the profit picture *looks much better* than under the general purchasing power equity concept.

In the long run shrinking dollar volume can jeopardize the continuity of the enterprise for two major reasons. In the first place if management and key personnel feel that their progress and ambitions are thwarted by the company's lack of progress, they may seek more promising employment elsewhere. Another danger to the continuity of the company is the fact that most, if not all, of the products subject to technological price decreases have an elastic demand and if the company cannot fill its part of the increased demand, the competition will do so, thus gradually reducing the company's relative market position.

The conservation of the shareholders' equity on the basis of the general purchasing power appears to be a better guarantee for the continuity of the enterprise. But it may be the second consideration — the wish to show a better profit picture to the public and to the shareholders, present as well as future — that tempts the company to change its viewpoint.

The danger to the continuity of the enterprise is evident. However, this may be offset by retaining a substantial part of the "distributable" profit for purposes of growth and expansion. It cannot be denied that it sounds more palatable to say first to shareholders, "See what a nice profit your company has made" and subsequently, "But it would not be in your interests to pay it all out because we need a part of it to enable the company to grow." Since most companies seem to be following this more palatable policy, one cannot blame the exception for joining the majority.

Holding Gains Concept

The "holding gains" concept would lead to the same profit as the "specific purchasing power equity concept" in our example, since no monetary assets or liabilities were involved. But if they were, the outcome would be different, since holding gains emanate only from the revaluation of the physical assets, whereas the equity concept also takes into account the balance of monetary assets and liabilities.

8.2 Companies With Foreign Assets and Income

It is not the intention to explain in this section how the financial statements of companies with foreign subsidiaries should be consolidated, but only to make a few observations with respect to the valuation of foreign assets and subsidiaries. Of course the current value concept applies here too.

There are two basic ways of proceeding with this type of valuation — the *investors' viewpoint* and the *integral viewpoint*. The latter considers foreign operations as an integral part of the home operations, like divisions or departments.

The Investors' Viewpoint

The investors' viewpoint must certainly be followed when the foreign activities are not controlled by the company. The type of interest may range from passive investments in securities or other assets to active participation in foreign entitites. The home company may have several interests such as trade in goods and services but no effective control over the activities involved.

As with other assets, the valuation principle of "market value and net proceeds, whichever is lower" applies here as well. From the investors' viewpoint the foreign assets, comprising all assets except those in which the home company has a controlling interest, should be valued as follows:

1. *Marketable assets: at market price*
   If the price is quoted in a foreign currency, it would be this price converted into dollars at the current rate of exchange. A problem arises if the net proceeds cannot be transferred to the home country due to monetary restrictions. In this case the current value should be based on the present value of the *transferable part* of the income from the asset.

2. *Non-marketable assets,* such as a minority interest in a foreign company: at the *present value* of the *expected income* from the company during the time this income is expected to flow

Income may comprise such items as dividends, royalties, and licence fees. Dividends from well-managed companies may be expected to flow indefinitely. The other types of income are generally for a limited time as stipulated in relative agreements. In calculating the present value the duration of the various income flows should be taken into account. It is an open question whether retained earnings should be taken into account as well. If it may be safely assumed that retained earnings will eventually increase the foreign company's income and dividend payments, it would appear to be justified to include the retained part of the income in the valuation of the assets.

The Integral Viewpoint

If the foreign company is *controlled* by the home company, two methods of valuation are available. As with local subsidiaries, the parent company could consider the foreign company as an *integral* part of its own operations, in which case the current value of the shares in that company could be based on the current value of its assets. If a third party has a minority interest, a percentage proportionate to the minority interest should be deducted from the current value of its assets to find the current value of the shares held by the parent company. Providing the currency of the subsidiary's country is not subject to transfer restrictions, the current value of the shares can be converted into dollars at the official rate of exchange.

The other method is to value the shares in the same way as the shares in a minority holding as described earlier in this section, namely, on the basis of the present value of the income the parent company expects to receive in future years. The final answer is the lower of the two, the intrinsic value based on the current value of the subsidiary's assets or the present value of future income from the subsidiary. The latter valuation may well be lower in those cases where the transfer of dividends and other payments of the subsidiary to the parent company is subject to monetary restrictions.

8.3   Differential Costs and Current Values

In Sections 1.5 and 1.6 it was implied that inventories of goods should be valued at *full costs* based on current values. The term "full costs" requires further definition, because sometimes it may be more appropriate to value a part of the inventory at less than full costs, that is, at *differential costs,* not only for the balance sheet but also for pricing policies and planning.

Full Cost Concept

Full or "integral" costs, under the current value concept based on the principles of continuity and normality, apply to goods either purchased or manufactured, under normal conditions for sale in a normal market and at a normal activity level of the organization. As such full costs include the cost of all resources used in the production of the goods to the state which they are in at the time of valuation, either during the production process, at balance sheet time or in a completely finished state at the time of sale. The cost of *used resources* in this context includes not only the costs of those resources which can be directly identified with the products involved, such as direct materials and direct labour but also an appropriate share of the costs of all company functions which have contributed, directly or indirectly, to the production of these products. In other words, full cost compromises both direct and indirect costs. How the indirect costs are allocated or prorated to the various products belongs to the art of cost accounting and is not a subject of this book.

Costs accumulate with each stage of the production process until the product is finished, inspected, packed and in a technical sense, ready for sale. Costs incurred by the company beyond this point, including the costs of acquiring sales orders and subsequently the costs of distribution, are conventionally not added to the value of the product but rather deducted from the proceeds of the sales. Therefore, these selling costs do not play a role in the valuation process. For asset valuation purposes the inventories of materials, work-in-process in successive states, semi-finished products, finished products, unpacked, packed and so on, are valued at the full costs accumulated at the various stages. For pricing policies the full cost of the finished products ready for sale, as well as the full appropriate selling costs, are relevant.

Many enterprises, subject to regular seasonal fluctuations in production or in sales or in both, may establish their capacity in terms of facilities and key personnel on the maximum load level in order to be in a position to take advantage of the seasonally high supplies or demands. As a result the available capacity is underloaded at regular intervals. Since this is considered to be normal and unavoidable, the capacity costs must be absorbed by the average load or *normal activity level*. The costs of idle capacity become part of the normal product unit costs.

Differential (or Additional) Cost Concept

If a company in this situation has an opportunity without risk to the basic business volume to acquire additional orders emanating from different markets, such as export or private brand markets, during the periods that the facilities are underloaded, then the *costs of the additional volume* are equal to the *additional costs*. Stated in another way, the cost of the additional business is the *differential* between the total cost and the costs at the normal activity level. The following example may be used as an illustration:

	Standard cost per unit	Differential cost per unit
Direct materials	$20	$20
Other variable costs	10	10
(freight, power, expense materials, etc.)		
Labour costs	10	10
Fixed manufacturing overheads	15	—
Total production costs	$55	$40
Selling costs	15	5
Total costs	$70	$45

If this company as a matter of policy does not lay off its personnel during the off-season periods, the differential costs may even be lower. The total differential costs per unit now become the basis to quote selling prices for the additional market. The inventories of the additional work-in-process and finished products should be valued at the differential cost level of $40 for a finished product in this example.

Accounting Problem

There may be an accounting problem when the basic and the additional volume consists of identical products and cannot be segregated in the stores. The solution in this case is to value the entire production at the same cost price, in this example $55, and to credit the difference in cost of $15 per unit of the additional production volume to a separate account, where it is held as a valuation adjustment to the inventory account. At the time of sale $15 per unit of the additional sales volume can then be transferred to "cost of sales."

Make-or-Buy Decisions

In make-or-buy decisions differential costs also enter the picture. For instance, when the company in the above example can buy the same product for $38 and save $40 either by laying off personnel or transferring them to another department where they can be usefully employed, then it is more economical to buy and to stop the production. However, if the labour costs, for some reason, cannot be reduced by more than $2 per unit, then it is more economical to continue the production. In both cases the current value decreases to $38 being the lower of cost and market price. In an accounting sense this means that of the labour and overhead costs, only $8 is absorbed leaving an unfavourable performance variance of $17 per unit.

8.4 Summary and Conclusions

A synopsis of the more important principles and considerations, as previously discussed in this book, pertinent to the process of designing an accounting system to account for inflation is as follows:

1. For a "going concern" revenues must be sufficient to:
    (i) Provide the interested parties, which include shareholders, managers and personnel, with an income that is economically adequate.
    (ii) Replace the used resources.

2. The *value* of the resources (assets) of an enterprise, based on *continuity*, is not the historical price that was paid for them, but the current price that has to be paid to replace them.

3. *Total profit* on a transaction is the difference between the proceeds and the historical costs. This applies to an isolated, single "one shot" deal, such as building a house or speculation in commodity futures, when replacement of used resources is *not intended*.

4. However, when replacement of used resources is intended, which is virtually always the case in a going concern, the total (or "nominalistic") profit on a transaction breaks up into two distinct parts:
    (i) The difference between the proceeds and the current value, which is the *transaction profit* or *operating profit*,
    (ii) The difference between the current value and the historical costs, which is the *holding gain* or *holding loss*.

5. In an enterprise based on continuity, the *current value* of the completed transaction represents the amount that is *committed* to replace, reproduce or renew the resources used up for the transaction. For this reason, the difference between the current value and the historical cost, in a going concern, is neither a profit (in times of rising prices) nor a loss (in times of falling prices), but a "holding" gain or loss.

6. Holding gains, occurring in periods of *rising* prices, cannot be paid out without affecting the continuity of the enterprise. Only the operating profit is available for distribution; that is for the payment of dividends and income taxes. On the other hand, in times of *falling* prices, when the current value drops below the historical cost, the unfavourable difference, or *holding loss*, should not reduce the operating profit, but rather be charged to earlier holding gains.

7. If, for some reason, the volume of business would be reduced to a new "normal" level, the holding gains attributable to the reduction of the non-monetary assets, are no longer committed to conserve the continuity of the enterprise and may therefore be considered as distributable profit. This conforms with the principle of Point 3, in that the volume reduction is not intended to be replaced and consequently does not require the conservation of corresponding funds.

8. When *physical* (or non-monetary) assets are temporarily *lower* than normal, as a result of which non-monetary assets are temporarily converted into *monetary assets*, which in times of rising prices are subject to a loss in purchasing power, a *provision* should be made to offset this loss in order to conserve the capital funds at a level that in due course is adequate to bring the assets up again to the normal level. This phenomenon may occur with fixed assets when replacement of worn out assets and amortization (on account of used "contributions") are not synchronized, in which case there is an *amortization gap*. It may also happen with inventories of materials and finished products, due to seasonal fluctuations or supply problems.

9. Losses due to amortization or inventory gaps may be avoided by a *financial structure* of the enterprise in which fluctuations in the non-monetary assets are synchronized with fluctuations in the capital funds from third parties, for example by long term loans the repayment of which is arranged to coincide with the amortization of the assets involved, and by bank or suppliers' credits for the financing of seasonal fluctuations in inventories.

10. If one is of the opinion that the *assets* are the *source of income* for the enterprise, the *holding gains concept*, accumulating in periods of inflation the value differences between the assets at current values and the assets at historical costs, is the answer to the problem of how to account for inflation, how to determine the distributable income and how to conserve the purchasing power in order to continue the enterprise on the basis of the same volume throughout the years. A part of this concept is that provisions are made for amortization and inventory gaps when they occur.

11. Closely related to this concept is the *equity concept* based on the *specific purchasing power* of the non-monetary assets. In this concept the *assets* as well as the *shareholders' equity* are carried at current values with the equity being adjusted by the same rate of price level changes as the non-monetary assets. This concept has the advantage over the basic holding gains concept in that a loss of purchasing power on the monetary assets, regardless of whether these assets arose from

amortization or inventory gaps or otherwise, is automatically taken into account. However, this advantage applies only to the extent that the enterprise is financed by equity funds.

12. If one is of the opinion that the *shareholders' equity* should be considered as the source of income the equity should be carried at the current value based on the *general rate of inflation*, as indicated by the Consumer Price Index or the GNE Implicit Price Index. In this case, losses may arise when the specific price level increases of the assets are lower than the general price level increases; this certainly happens with products subject to technological price decreases, as mentioned in Section 8.1. When this equity concept is adhered to, the equity funds will be adequate to finance a *stable dollar volume* of business. This of course involves a larger quantity, if the specific price level rise lags behind the general price level rise.

13. *Standard costs*, in manufacturing enterprises, are an excellent application of current values if based on the three principles of continuity, normality and fairness, and if they conform to the three dimensions of quantities, prices and time. The time dimension involves the inclusion of an interest charge in the costs. In the event that the prices and rates, at which the quantities of materials, labour, services and interest have been valued, are subject to fluctuations beyond a degree that would tend to render the standard costs inadequate for decision-making, these should either be revised or be adjusted by means of price indices, whichever method is more economical.

14. In designing an accounting system the *requirements of management* for decision-making, for performance control and for planning should have priority over all other objectives. The requirements for shareholders and other interested parties as well as for income tax purposes, however important, should take second place.

15. The accounting procedure should be designed in such a way that both the balance sheet and the income statement are the result of one and the same process. This provides for an automatic analysis of all changes in assets and liabilities as well as in the shareholders' equity.

16. In order to fulfill its objective the management accounting system of a going concern must be responsive to the concept of current values based on the *three principles of continuity, normality and equity.* These *principles* apply to all types of enterprises. They explain *why*, while *rules, conventions and procedures* which may be applied differently from one enterprise to another stipulate *how* things are to be accounted for.

Chapter 9

APPLICATIONS OF CURRENT VALUE CONCEPTS

9.1 Review

There is a growing awareness amongst business leaders, economists, investors, financial analysts and accountants that the conventional type of financial information, based on historical costs, does not enable them to form a sound judgement about the financial position and the performance of business enterprises. This is evident from the increasing amount of literature being published on this subject in recent years, mainly in the form of articles in professional magazines and the business press. Most of the authors of this literature, while accepting inflation as a permanent phenomenon, recommend the *supplementation* of conventional information with current relevant information rather than the substitution of current values for historical costs.

The greater part of the literature is predominantly concerned with the annual financial statements for shareholders and only a small part with the requirements for management. A laudable exception is the recognition of the importance of the latter by Howard Ross in a book that concentrates mainly on the problems of published statements:

> The production of satisfactory statements for management in today's conditions of increasing complexity has become the chief accounting problem in large corporations and is entitled to first priority over all other accounting requirements. The accounting system should be basically designed to produce the information that management needs. Custodial accounting, however important, comes after management accounting. The accountant must think first of the requirements of good statements for management. Once these have been produced, it is a relatively simple matter to make the necessary adjustments to produce satisfactory custodial statements.[1]

The ways recommended in various articles of how to provide the shareholders with additional information to render the annual statements relevant to the current situation vary greatly. Some suggest providing the additional information in footnotes to the financial statements. Others suggest providing the statements with double columns, one column for the historical figures, the other column for current values. A few abandon the historical cost basis altogether and substitute current values.

A great deal of attention is given to the valuation problems involved in the updating of the value of fixed assets and inventories. In this respect various methods are advocated, such as:

1. Appraisals for land, buildings, machinery and equipment.
2. Price level restatements, based on historical costs, updated to the current price level by means of a price index, either by using:
   2.1 A general price index reflecting the change in the purchasing power of the dollar, or
   2.2 A specific price index reflecting the change in the price level of the specific group of assets involved.
3. Replacement cost; the current market price for purchased assets.
4. Reproduction cost; the current costs involved in reproducing the asset. This is a variant of replacement cost applicable to manufactured goods.
5. Realizable value; either
   5.1 Direct realizable value; the resale price less costs to be incurred to effect the sale, or
   5.2 Indirect realizable value; the value of an asset based on the future revenues it will generate.

In North America very few companies have experimented with the publication of supplementary price level information in their annual financial statements. Thus far no organized efforts have been undertaken by professional associations or governmental bodies to make a proposal to change "generally accepted accounting principles" in the direction of price level accounting or current value accounting. The Securities and Exchange Commission and the American Institute of Certified Public Accountants, probably the most influential bodies with respect to financial reporting in the United States of America, have continued to support generally accepted accounting principles based on historical costs.

Although the Accounting Principles Board of the AICPA in a pronouncement in 1969 confirmed the usefulness of including general price level information as supplementary information in financial statements, at the same time it stated that such information was not needed to give a fair presentation of financial position and results of operations in conformity with generally accepted accounting principles in the USA. As a result few companies in the USA and Canada have seen fit to do more than comment about the effects of inflation in their annual reports. The new full-time Financial Accounting Standards Board, which was formed in the USA in 1973 under influential private sponsorship including the AICPA, in response to a growing public dissatisfaction with financial reporting generally, has added price level changes to its list of topics under study. Undoubtedly recent acceleration in the rates of inflation in North America have helped to emphasize the inadequacy of financial reporting based on historical costs. As yet, it is too early to tell whether this board will recommend any move towards price level accounting or current value accounting.

In the United Kingdom, where the rate of inflation has been higher than in North America, greater cognizance has been taken of the inadequacies of conventional financial presentation based on historical costs. In the past few years a number of UK companies have added supplementary information to their annual statements, either in footnotes to the statements or in additional columns. A development of great interest took place in January, 1973, when the Accounting Standards Steering Committee of The Institute of Chartered Accountants in England and Wales issued a proposal for a new standard accounting practice entitled "Accounting for Changes in the Purchasing Power of Money". It was proposed that companies listed on a recognized stock exchange publish their annual statements accompanied by supplementary information showing the effects of price level changes on both the financial position and income. Although substantial support for some form of inflation accounting quickly developed after the issuance of this proposal, there was controversy over the method proposed, as some people expressed a preference for current value accounting. In July, 1973, as the controversy heightened, the government appointed a special committee of its own to enquire into the subject since it realized the serious effects which current purchasing power accounting could have on its policies, especially with regard to inflation and taxation. In response to the accelerating rate of inflation and the length of time that would be required by the government committee to complete its investigation, the Accounting Standards Steering Committee felt impelled to publish a "provisional standard" in May, 1974, confirming its original proposal. Most companies in the United Kingdom are expected to conform to this provisional standard although they will not be obliged to do so. In Section 9.3 this proposal is reviewed in more detail because of its obvious importance.

It is likely that continental Europe, particularly the Netherlands, is the most advanced in the application of current value accounting. A recent article in *Accountancy*[2] refers to a survey concerning the accounting practices applied in 1967 to property and depreciation by 259 of the 289 commercial and industrial Dutch companies listed on the Amsterdam Stock Exchange. This survey shows that approximately half of the companies give some recognition to current values in their financial statements, and 39 companies have stated their property at current values and based depreciation on current values. One of the largest of these is N.V. Philips' Gloeilampenfabrieken which introduced the current value concept (or the "replacement value theory" as it is called in the Netherlands) into its costing system as early as 1936. Today the information for both shareholders and for management is based on current values. In the next section, the Philips system is reviewed in some detail and a reprint of the company's latest financial statements with explanatory notes on the principles of valuation and the principles of calculating income is included in an appendix.

9.2   N.V. Philips' Gloeilampenfabrieken

Philips is a multinational concern with its head office in Eindhoven, the Netherlands, and with subsidiaries in most countries of the free world. The concern manufactures a great variety of electrical and electronic products. According to its 1973 annual report Philips employs 402,000 persons, of which 97,000 are in the Netherlands. Total sales in 1973 amounted to 22.5 billion guilders (over 8 billion dollars) with assets of 24 billion guilders (approximately 8.6 billion dollars) and a shareholders' equity of 8.4 billion guilders (3 billion dollars).

Information extracted from the Philips' financial statements for 1973 is shown in the appendix to this section on pages 136 through 141 for reference purposes in conjunction with the comments which follow. This information includes:

1. Combined Statement of Financial Position (after income appropriation).

2. Combined Statement of Results (before income appropriation).

3. Explanatory Notes to the Combined Statements, including
   3.1 Principles of valuation
   3.2 Principles of calculating profit.

4. Calculation of Net Profit based on American Accounting Principles.

From the latter statement it is evident that the Philips' method of determining income results in a lower profit than would be the case under the American accounting rules, which are based on historical costs.

Introduction of the Current Value Concept

Philips introduced the current value concept in 1936 after the devaluation of the guilder in order to provide management with a realistic basis for its pricing policies, for make-or-buy decisions as well as for profit control, budgeting and planning. Because of the great number of products, parts and components, the standard cost prices used for performance control and for inventory control were revised yearly, whereas, for sales pricing and profit control, the standard costs were adjusted to the current price level (replacement cost level) by means of price indices whenever significant changes occurred. For most products the price indices were calculated for product groups or sub-groups which were homogeneous with respect to the price level changes of their component parts. Prototypes, which were considered to be representative for the relevant groups, were used in most cases to facilitate quick revision of the price indices. For the periodic calculation of the price indices, some forecasting was done with respect to the probable level of prices during the period in which the price indices were to be used. In other words, the price indices did not actually represent the current price level on a specific date, but anticipated the average price level during a forthcoming period and as such contained a certain amount of speculation.

The concept of current values was gradually introduced into the accounting system. Due to disruption caused by World War II, it was not until some time after the end of the war that this concept was applied completely in the valuation of the assets, in the internal and external financial reporting, and in the accounting system. At present, there is no difference, except in details, between the information provided for managerial purposes and that given to the shareholders. Taxable income is calculated separately from the accounts, in accordance with existing tax laws in the various countries in which Philips operates.

Philips' view of the current value concept is that the assets, rather than the shareholders' equity, are the source of income. Consequently the *equity proper* is not subjected to a revaluation due to changes in the purchasing power of the guilder. The revaluation is limited to the assets. A gain is credited to a "revaluation surplus" account whereas a revaluation loss, if any, is charged to this account. The revaluation surplus account is part of the group of equity accounts (see the balance sheet of Philips in the appendix to this chapter). The Philips' application of the current value concept approaches the "holding gains" concept as explained in Section 1.4. A few peculiarities in the Philips' system are worth noting.

Valuation of Fixed Assets and Inventories

Fixed assets are normally revalued once per year if the price level has changed more than a certain percentage, either item by item or by using price indices for groups of similar assets or groups of complementary assets, which are homogeneous with respect to changes in price levels. In isolated cases, such as assets which constitute independent sources of income or assets for which a resale value is available (for example, office buildings and transportation equipment), the indirect or direct proceeds, as explained in Section 1.6 and 5.6, may be used as a basis for valuation in the event that replacement cost is not applicable, not available or higher. The amount of change in the value of the fixed assets is transferred to the revaluation surplus account.

Since Philips considers itself, for the entire concern, to be very close to the "ideal complex" situation, as mentioned in Section 5.5, where the amortization of the fixed assets on a current value basis equals the cost of replacement of worn out and discarded fixed assets, no additional provisions are deemed to be necessary as the case would be in the event of an amortization gap.

The valuation of the inventories is based on the same rules as the fixed assets, namely, on the current value. A change in the price level is transferred to the revaluation surplus account. However, before 1971 the revaluation surplus account was also credited for the loss of purchasing power of the capital funds devoted to the inventories caused by the fact that as a consequence of the technological price decrease of the Philips products the price level of the Philips products lagged behind the general price level. Section 8.1 explains the effects of technological price decreases more in general.

Whereas from 1971, the capital funds devoted to both fixed assets and inventories were adjusted in accordance with the specific price level, or specific rate of inflation, before 1971 different rules were applied; the specific rate of inflation to the capital funds invested in fixed assets and the general rate of inflation to the capital funds invested in inventories.

Excess of Liabilities over Monetary Assets

It is considered to be part of the replacement value theory, as adhered to in the Netherlands, to charge the income account for the loss of purchasing power of the capital funds devoted to an excess, if any, of monetary assets over monetary liabilities. As Philips' monetary liabilities for the concern as a whole exceed the monetary assets considerably, as shown in the condensed balance sheet below, no provision for this purpose was necessary.

Balance Sheet as at December 31, 1973

Physical assets	15.5	Equity accounts	9.5
Monetary assets	8.7	Liabilities	14.7
	24.2		24.2

Amounts in billions of guilders.

In 1973 Philips credited the revaluation surplus account with 578 million guilders. Accordingly, the specific purchasing power of the funds devoted to physical assets diminished in 1973 by 3.7%. If Philips had followed the equity concept (See Sections 1.4 and 3.2) based on a specific rate of inflation of 3.7% the revaluation adjustment account would have shown the following figures for 1973:

1. Revaluation gains on assets   578 million guilders

2. Charges for the revaluation of
    the equity (3.7% of 9.5 billion guilders)   351 million guilders

3. Balance   227 million guilders

This balance represents the gain of 3.7% on the excess of liabilities over monetary assets, that is 6 billion guilders, which under the equity concept, based on the specific purchasing power principle, may be considered as income.

Latent Tax Liabilities

Another change in reporting income was made in 1971 with respect to the *latent tax liabilities.* Before 1971 the latent tax liability was charged to the income account, but from 1971 was charged to the revaluation surplus account, thus to the equity accounts. For 1973, the charge amounted to 280 million guilders, reducing the revaluation surplus of 1973 from 578 to 298 million guilders.

Summary

The Philips method of accounting may be considered as the most advanced when compared to other known applications, not only because of the complete adherence to current values, which have replaced the historical costs in the accounts, but also because of the fact that the same information is used both for shareholders (quarterly reports) and for management.

The only point that may be criticized is that Philips does not adjust shareholders' equity in accordance with the *general rate of inflation.* This has been considerably higher in recent years than the specific rate of inflation, which as noted above amounted to 3.7% in 1973. On the other hand Philips consistently retains a substantial part of net income, 61% in 1973 and 62% in 1972, up from 32% to 51% in previous years, enabling the company to finance a part of the growing business volume.

Appendix

N. V. Philips' Gloeilampenfabrieken

Combined Statement
of Financial Position

	1973		1972	
Property, plant and equipment				
Replacement value	15,758.6		14,105.8	
Depreciation	−7,401.1	8,357.5	−6,518.5	7,587.3
Intangible assets		—		—
Investments in non-consolidated subsidiaries and associated companies		609.8		578.2
Sundry non-current assets		690.5		622.4
Stocks				
Factory stocks	3,591.7		2,905.8	
Advance payments by customers	−403.9		−421.3	
	3,187.8		2,484.5	
Commercial stocks	3,242.5	6,430.3	2,938.7	5,423.2
Accounts receivable				
Trade debtors	6,415.7		5,737.8	
Discounted bills	−403.8		−392.6	
	6,011.9		5,345.2	
Other accounts receivable	490.8		445.0	
Prepaid expenses	349.2	6,851.9	316.2	6,106.4
Liquid assets				
Marketable securities	223.1		195.2	
Cash at bank and in hand	1,024.0	1,247.1	1,618.4	1,813.6
		24,187.1		22,131.1

Amounts in millions of guilders

	1973		1972	
Shareholders' equity interest				
Ordinary share capital	1,636.3		1,274.1	
Share premium account	280.1		619.3	
Retained profit	4,520.2		3,821.0	
Revaluation surplus	2,013.9	8,450.5	1,715.8	7,430.2
Minority interests		1,022.6		907.0
Sundry provisions				
Long-term provisions	2,554.7		2,092.7	
Short-term provisions	899.1	3,453.8	744.3	2,837.0
Long-term liabilities				
Convertible debenture loans	742.4		773.1	
Other debenture loans	548.1		611.7	
Other long-term liabilities	2,460.9	3,751.4	2,722.1	4,106.9
Current liabilities				
Banks	1,886.8		2,256.5	
Accounts payable	3,250.8		2,716.9	
Tax on profit	994.8		638.8	
Accrued expenses	1,127.4	7,259.8	1,043.6	6,655.8
Profit available for distribution	347.2		270.6	
Interim dividend made payable in December	−98.2	249.0	−76.4	194.2
		24,187.1		22,131.1

Appendix

N. V. Philips' Gloeilampenfabrieken

**Combined Statement
of Results**

	1973		1972	
Sales		22,562.8		19,924.5
Costs and expenses:				
Cost of sales	−15,484.8		−13,752.2	
Selling and general expenses	−4,481.2	−19,966.0	−4,197.4	−17,949.6
Trading Profit		2,596.8		1,974.9
Other income and charges:				
Interest paid	−520.7		−537.6	
Interest received	120.7		99.3	
	−400.0		−438.3	
Extraordinary income	88.1		99.9	
Extraordinary charges	−356.0	−667.9	−172.6	−511.0
Profit before tax		1,928.9		1,463.9
Tax on profit		−962.9		−719.3
Profit after tax		966.0		744.6
Share in net profit of non-consolidated companies		61.4		62.7
Group profit		1,027.4		807.3
Minority interests		−128.3		−90.1
Net profit		899.1		717.2

Amounts in millions of guilders

Explanatory Notes to
the Combined Statements

These statements combine the consolidated data of N.V. Philips' Gloeilampenfabrieken and those of the United States Philips Trust.

Principles of valuation

Property, plant and equipment

These assets and their depreciation are valued on the basis of replacement value. Changes in the replacement value are credited or charged to Revaluation Surplus.

Intangible assets

Intangible assets are shown in the balance sheet at no value.

Investments in non-consolidated subsidiaries and associated companies

Non-consolidated investments are valued at their net tangible asset value, determined in accordance with the principles adopted in these annual accounts.

Sundry non-current assets

These assets are valued at purchase price or at estimated realizable value, whichever is the lower.

Stocks

Stocks are valued at replacement value or at estimated realizable value, whichever is the lower. Changes in replacement value are credited or charged to Revaluation Surplus. The provision for the risk of obsolescence is deducted from the total figure for stocks. Profits arising from transactions within the Philips organization are eliminated.

Accounts receivable

Accounts receivable are shown at nominal value, less the provision for the risk of bad debts.

Liquid assets

Securities are valued at purchase price or at their listed stock exchange price at the end of the financial year, whichever is the lower. Shares in N.V. Gemeenschappelijk Bezit van Aandeelen Philips' Gloeilampenfabrieken and debentures of N.V. Philips' Gloeilampen- fabrieken and of their associated companies are included at par.

Minority interests

Minority interests in consolidated subsidiaries are valued on the basis of net tangible asset value, determined in accordance with the principles adopted in these annual accounts.

Sundry provisions

These provisions do not relate to specific assets; they are formed to meet commitments and risks connected with the course of business. Pension provisions are included under this heading at present value.

Long-term and current liabilities

These liabilities are taken up at nominal value.

Replacement value

The replacement value is determined on the basis of the price trends of the various assets, making use inter alia of indices. Transfers to Revaluation Surplus pursuant to changes in the replacement value are made after deduction of latent tax liabilities.

Foreign currencies

In the Combined Statement of Financial Position amounts in foreign currency are converted into guilders at the official exchange rates applicable on the balance sheet date, unless circumstances, as, for instance, the trend of the purchasing power of the currency concerned, call for the adoption of a lower rate.

Exchange differences due to the conversion into guilders of property, plant and equipment and stocks are offset against Revaluation Surplus in the relevant country.

Exchange differences due to the conversion in guilders of nominal assets and liabilities are credited or charged to Profit and Loss Account.

In the Combined Statement of Results, sales and income in foreign currencies are converted at the rates applicable in the relevant periods.

The balance of the relevant profit and loss account is converted at the end of the year at the rates applied in the Combined Statement of Financial Position. The resultant difference is credited or charged to Profit and Loss Account.

Principles of calculating profit

- The sales figure represents the net proceeds from goods and services supplied to third parties.
- Depreciation of property, plant and equipment is calculated on the basis of fixed percentages of the replacement value.
- Consumption of raw materials and the other elements in the cost of sales are also calculated on the basis of replacement value.
- Provisions for risks inherent in operations are built up in proportion to the volume of business.
- Expenditure on research, development, patents, licences, copyrights and concessions is charged in the current year to Profit and Loss Account. Net amounts paid in excess of the net tangible asset value for the acquisition of participations in any year are similarly charged in that year to Profit and Loss Account.
- For taxes on profit provisions are made on the basis of the profit figure determined in accordance with our principles of valuation, which implies that latent taxes are taken into account. In so far as the cost of sales differs from historical cost owing to the use of the replacement value, the tax payable on that difference is charged to the provision made for latent taxes at the time of revaluation.

Calculation of Net Profit based on American Accounting Principles

The accounting principles applied by N.V. Philips' Gloeilampenfabrieken in calculating profit differ in some respects from those generally accepted in the United States of America. The main differences are:

- Depreciation on property, plant and equipment is based on the replacement value of the assets concerned.
- Stocks are in general valued at replacement value. This value is used for determining the cost of sales.
- In so far as the cost of sales differs from historical cost owing to the use of the replacement value, the tax payable on that difference is charged to the provision made for latent taxes at the time of revaluation.
- Net amounts paid in excess of the net tangible asset value for the acquisition of participations in any year are charged in that year to Profit and Loss Account.

- The share of profit due to the Supervisory Board, Management and Officers and to employees, in accordance with the Articles of Association, is not charged to Profit and Loss Account.

An attempt is made below to estimate what adjustment to net profit would be required if the principles generally accepted in the United States were applied, based on the first-in first-out method for the consumption of goods and using a write-off period of five years for net payments in respect of goodwill.

	in millions of guilders	in millions of U.S. dollars *
Net profit 1973 shown in the Combined Statement of Results	899.1	321.1
Deduct: Profit-sharing with Supervisory Board, Management and Officers and with employees	−52.6	−18.8
Adjustment of net profit on the basis of accounting principles generally accepted in the United States	71.8	25.6
Adjusted net profit	918.3	327.9
Number of ordinary shares of f 10 of N.V. Philips' Gloeilampenfabrieken outstanding at 31 December 1973	163,628,632	
Per ordinary share of f 10 of N.V. Philips' Gloeilampenfabrieken:		
Adjusted net profit	f 5.61	$ 2.00
Dividend	f 1.80	$ 0.64

Assuming conversion of all outstanding convertible debentures, the adjusted net profit per ordinary share would be f 5.23 ($ 1.87).

If the method of historical cost had been applied in the past, it is estimated that the item Revaluation Surplus as shown in the Combined Statement of Financial Position as at 31 December 1973, would have appeared as follows:

	in millions of guilders	in millions of U.S. dollars *
Addition to retained profit	1,199.3	428.3
Deduction from property, plant and equipment and stocks	814.6	290.9
	2,013.9	719.2

*Converted at the rate of f 2.80 per U.S. dollar.

9.3   Progress in England

The Accounting Standards Steering Committee of The Institute of Chartered Accountants in England and Wales has issued a proposed statement of standard accounting practice, entitled "Accounting for Changes in the Purchasing Power of Money".[3] Although the proposed changes in the accounting practice do not aim at providing management with information for its day-to-day decision-making process, the proposal must be considered as a *breakthrough in the conventional accounting philosophy* in that a body as important as The Institute of Chartered Accountants in England and Wales now considers it a necessity to provide the shareholders with information that neutralizes the effects of inflation, in addition to the conventional information based on historical costs. The proposed changes in accounting practice recognizes the fact that information based on historical costs is at least inadequate and possibly wrong. This recognition may provide the right atmosphere to carry the development of the accounting system beyond the proposed first step and to include the requirements for management as well. To this end the preceding chapters of this book may be helpful.

The proposed accounting standard would apply to the published annual accounts of companies having a quotation on a recognized stock exchange; however, the accounting standard is recommended for other types of business as well (Point 32 of the proposal). The main features of the proposed accounting standard are (Point 11):

1. Companies will continue to keep their records and present their *basic* annual accounts in historical pounds; that is, in terms of the value of the pound at the time of each transaction or revaluation.

2. In addition, all quoted companies should present to their shareholders a *supplementary* statement in terms of the value of the pound at the end of the period to which the accounts relate.

3. The conversion of the figures in the *basic* accounts into the figures in the *supplementary* statement should be by means of a general index of the purchasing power of the pound.

The index to be used in the conversion process should be the Consumer Price Index produced by the Central Statistical Office (Point 23). The method proposed (the "general purchasing power method") shows the effects on annual accounts of inflation only; that is, of changes in the general purchasing power or value of money. It does not show changes in value due to changes in other factors such as technology or market pressures, and therefore does not introduce other concepts such as replacement costs or current values (Point 8).

In converting from basic historical cost accounts to supplementary current purchasing power statements for any particular period, the proposal states that:

1. Monetary items in the balance sheet at the end of period remain the same (Point 20).

2. Non-monetary items are increased in proportion to the inflation that has occurred since their acquisition or revaluation (and conversely, reduced in times of deflation) (Point 20).

3. In the conversion process, after increasing non-monetary items by the amount of inflation, it is necessary to apply the test of lower of cost (expressed in pounds of current purchasing power) and net realisable value to relevant current assets (stocks, for example) and further to adjust the figures if necessary. Similarly, after restating fixed assets in terms of pounds of current purchasing power, the question of the value to the business needs to be reviewed in that context and provision made if necessary (Point 21).

4. Holders of monetary assets lose general purchasing power during a period of inflation to the extent that any income from the assets does not adequately compensate for the loss; the converse applies to those having monetary liabilities. A company with a material excess on average over the year of long and short term debt (e.g. debentures and creditors) over debtors and cash will show, in its supplementary current purchasing power statement, a gain in purchasing power during the year (Point 17).

Comments

1. There seems to be an inconsistency between Point 8 and Point 21. Applying the rule of Point 8 literally, it would mean that the part of the shareholders' equity invested in non-monetary assets is revalued on the basis of the general rate of inflation. Applying the rule of Point 21 however, the adjustment of the equity approaches the *holding gains* concept (See Section 1.4) in that the equity is increased in times of rising prices by the difference between the historical costs and the "real" or "fair" values. The latter is defined as the lower of historical pounds converted to current pounds by the Consumer Price Index (which assumes that the price increase was the same for all commodities) and net realisable value or the value to the business. The application of the general purchasing power index to all non-monetary assets over a number of years may well lead to a distortion of the actual situation since the price movement of the various assets may vary substantially from the average price increase as indicated by the Consumer Price

Index. If the price increases of fixed assets and of materials and products lag behind the average price increases, then the financial position of the company involved is shown more favourably than it really is. A case in point is shown by the latest balance sheet of N.V. Philips' Gloeilampenfabrieken of the Netherlands as of December 31, 1973; this shows for the non-monetary assets a real revaluation gain of 578 million guilders over 1973, representing a price increase (or a *specific rate of inflation*) of 3.7% only, whereas the *general rate of inflation* in the Netherlands, as in many other countries of the Western World, amounted to 8% in 1973. It would, therefore, be more realistic to revalue the non-monetary assets on the basis of their real, fair or current values, for which purpose the lower of replacement (reproduction) cost and the net realisable value to the company seems to be the most appropriate choice.

2. It must be assumed from Point 17 of the proposal that purchasing power losses due to an excess of monetary assets over liabilities as well as gains due to an excess of liabilities over monetary assets must be taken into account in determining profit. As observed in Section 4.3, gains due to the financial structure of the enterprise, that is where there is an excess of liabilities over monetary assets, are not available for distribution because they may be committed to maintain the physical assets at a normal level.

3. The updating of the figures of previous years to make the successive years comparable is a good feature of the proposal.

4. Another worthwhile recommendation is contained in Point 22: "The supplementary current purchasing power statement can be no more than an approximation, and it is pointless to strive for over-elaborate precision."

Notes

1. Howard Ross: "The Elusive Art of Accounting". New York: The Ronald Press Company, 1966, page 115.
2. A.W. Knol, "Accounting in Holland" in *Accountancy*, January, 1973, pp. 32-38.
3. See *Exposure Draft ED8*, The Institute of Chartered Accountants in England and Wales, Chartered Accountants' Hall, Moorgate Place, London, England, January 17, 1973. All further quotations in this section are from the above-mentioned draft.

INDEX

Accounting
 for differential costs, 123
 system in manufacturing and
   service enterprises, 83-101
 system in trading enterprises, 35-62
Accounting method
 conventional, 25, 35
 custodial, 29, 103
 management (managerial), 1, 29,
   30, 103
Accounting Principles Board of the
   American Institute of Certified
   Public Accountants, 130
Accounting Standards Steering
   Committee of the Institute of
   Chartered Accountants in
   England and Wales, 131, 142
Accrual method of accounting, 15
Accuracy in accounting, 47
Additional (differential) costs, 16, 20,
   97, 123-125, 129
Allowance for
 amortization of fixed assets, 21, 75
 obsolescence, 23, 60, 61
 technological price decreases, 120
 losses of purchasing power on
   monetary assets, 79
Alternative investment opportu-
   nities, 4
Amortization gap, 10, 63-70, 77, 127
Annuity method of amortization, 21,
   23, 75
 variant to, 76
Applications of current value
   concepts, 129
Appraisals of assets, 21, 130

Balance sheet, based on
 current values, 8, 9, 11, 12, 37, 39,
   50, 53, 54, 56, 57
 historical costs, 8, 36
 lifo, 40
Bonds, 4
Book values, 3

Budgeting, 8, 19, 30
Buildings
 valuation of, 74
Business economics
 accounting principles based on, 30,
   126, 127

Calculation of price indices, 84-86
Capital gains, 3-6
Cash flow, 15
Comparative summary of the effects of
   the different concepts of profit, 63
Complementary assets
 valuation of, 22
Concept of
 costs, 15
 current value, 1-3, 31, 32
 profit, 6
Consumer Price Index (CPI), 1, 13, 51
Continuity principle, 2, 7, 8, 11, 12,
   17, 32
Continuous
 income, 2
 inflation, 5
Conventional method of accounting,
   25, 35
Corporate income taxes, 5, 27, 106
Cost allowance for
 amortization of fixed assets, 21, 75
 losses of purchasing power on
   monetary assets, 79
 obsolescence, 23, 60, 61
 technological price decreases, 120
Costing procedures, 17
Costs
 concept of, 15
 dimensions of, 17
 objectives of, 16
Current
 market price, 2, 20
 value, 1, 3
 value concept, 31-33
Current value method of accounting,
   26, 30

Current values
  and fluctuating inventories, 38
  and standard costs, 41
Custodial method of accounting, 29,
    35, 103
Custodial adjustment accounts, 110,
    116

Deferred income tax liabilities, 108
Depreciation gap (see Amortization
    gap)
Different costs for different purposes,
    16
Differential costs
  concept of, 124
  accounting of, 125
Differential costs and current values,
    123
Differential costs and prices, 16, 20,
    97, 123-125
Distributable profit, 8, 10, 12, 37
Dividend, 3-5

Earning power (profitability), 1, 4
Economic concept of costs, 18
Effects of inflation on
  income taxes, 27
  investment decisions, 24
  private enterprise, 2
  shareholders, 3
Equity concepts, 9, 11, 13, 33
Equity concept
  based on general rate of inflation,
      13, 64, 67, 69, 70
  based on specific rate of inflation,
      13, 64, 66, 69, 70
Excess of
  monetary assets over liabilities, 63
  liabilities over monetary assets, 63,
      134
Expansion, 16

Fair value, 3
Fairness principle in costing, 17, 32
Financial Accounting Standards
    Board, 130
Financing policy, 71
Financial position, 3
Financial results, 72, 90, 92
Financial structure and inflation, 51,
    80, 127
Fixed assets
  character of, 21
  contribution units of, 21, 74
  ideal complex of, 79, 133
Fixed assets and current values, 71
Fixed overheads, 16, 125
Foreign assets, 122

Foreign income, 122
Forward planning (see Planning)
Frequency of value adjustments, 61
Full (integral) costs, 16, 20, 124
Future proceeds a basis for valuation
    of assets, 81

General purchasing power (general
    rate of inflation), 33, 51, 64, 67,
    69, 70, 128
Going concern concept, 3, 17, 20, 126
Gross National Expenditure (GNE)
    Implicit Price Index, 13, 51

Historical costs, 2, 7, 17, 20, 27, 35,
    63-65, 68, 70
Holding gains, 7-9, 14, 30, 33, 50, 64,
    65, 68, 70, 126, 133

Ideal complex of capital assets, 79, 133
Imputed interest charge (see Interest)
Income concept, 2
Income taxes, 5, 27, 106
Index method, 22, 42, 44, 84, 85
Individual assets
  valuation of, 22
Inflation
  what is, 1
  losses on monetary assets, 50-79
  inflation-proof tax system, 29
Information for management
  prospective, 30, 31
  retrospective, 30
Institute of Chartered Accountants in
    England and Wales, 131, 143
Integral cost concept, 16, 124
Integrated system of accounts, 110
Integration of managerial and
    custodial accounting, 103
Interest charge in costs
  advantages of, 82
  principle of, 14, 17, 23, 71, 72
  rate of, 18
Interest payable, 18, 19, 72
Interim reporting, 54
Intrinsic value, 4
Inventory account based on
  current values, 36, 38
  historical costs, 35
  lifo, 40
  standard costs, 44
Inventory price level adjustment
    account, 53
Inventory gap, 63-70, 127

Labour
  performance variances, 92
  rate variances, 92, 95

Land
  costs, 72
  values, 21
Latent income tax liability, 106, 135
Lifetime variances on capital assets,
  14, 24, 82
Last-in, first-out (LIFO) rule, 38, 40, 41
Loss of purchasing power on monetary
  assets, 10, 12, 14, 29, 79

Machinery
  amortization, 74, 75
  valuation, 77, 81
Make-or-buy decision, 16, 125
Managerial (Management)
    accounting
  principles, 126, 127
  system, 1, 29, 30, 103
Marketable assets
  valuation of, 122
Minimum income concept, 2, 4
Monetary assets and liabilities, 9, 10,
  49, 63-70

Net proceeds
  as a basis for valuation, 3, 21, 81
  direct, 21
  indirect, 22
Nominal assets (see Monetary assets)
Nominal (nominalistic or total) profit,
  7, 8, 14, 15, 126
Non-marketable assets
  valuation of, 123
Normal activity (normal capacity),
  14, 17, 83
Normality
  principle of, 17, 32

Objective
  of enterprise, 2
  of costs, 16
Obsolete assets; Obsolescence, 21, 23,
  59-61
Operating profit; Operating results,
  7, 8, 14, 30, 126
Opportunity costs, 18
Overhead costs and current values, 99
Overhead variances, 95

Pay-out ratio, 4
Performance
  actual, 14, 31
  budgeted, 14, 31
  control, 14, 19, 84
  standard, 14, 31
  variances, 14, 31, 84
Philips Gloeilampenfabrieken,
  132-141

principles of valuation, 139, 140
principles of calculating profit, 140
Planning, 8, 16, 19, 24, 30
Present value, 21, 22, 25, 26, 81
Price leaders and price followers in
    private enterprise, 16
Price fluctuations (price level
    changes), 14, 19, 44, 45, 55, 84, 95
Price fluctuation absorption, 88, 90, 95
Price indices (indexes)
  application, 19
  calculation of
    in manufacturing, 84-86
    in trading, 42-44
    per group, 85
    per prototype, 85, 86
Price level restatement, 22, 130
Pricing policy, 16
Principle of
  continuity, 2, 17, 32
  fairness, 17, 32
  normality, 17, 32
Private enterprise
  effects of inflation on, 2
Private company, 6
Profit
  appropriation, 15, 71
  available for distribution, 8, 10, 12,
    37
  concept, 6
  control, 19
  determination, 15, 71
Profit centre concept, 96
Profitability (earning power), 1, 4
Profit and loss account based on
  current values, 37
  historical costs, 35
Provision for loss of purchasing
    power on
  monetary assets, 79, 127
Public company, 5
Purchasing power
  general rate of inflation, 33, 51, 64,
    67, 69, 70, 128
  specific rate of inflation, 33, 51, 64,
    69, 70, 127

Quarterly financial reports, 118

Rate of return, 28
Realizable value, 3
  direct, 21, 130
  indirect, 22, 130
Relevant values, 20
Replacement cost; Replacement price,
  3, 16, 17, 20, 130
Reproduction cost, 20, 130
Residual income, 14, 72

Revaluation adjustment account, 49,
    52, 54, 56, 59
Revaluation surplus, 8, 13
Revaluation results; revaluation
    variance, 13, 30, 52

Scrap, 21
Service industries and current values,
    101
Shareholders' equity (see Equity)
Shrinking business volume, 121
Source of income
    assets as, 11, 127
    equity as, 11, 127
Specific purchasing power (Specific
    rate of inflation), 33, 51, 64, 69,
    70, 120, 127
Speculation results, 10, 14, 31, 46
Standard costs
    advantages and disadvantages of, 41
    and accounting, 43
    and current values, 41, 128
    and fluctuating inventories, 46
    and price fluctuations, 19
    breakdown of operating results, 14
    in manufacturing, 83
    in trading enterprises, 43, 44
    types of, 16
Statements for income tax purposes,
    108
Strategic planning in investment
    decisions, 24
System designed for management
    accounting only, 103
System of accounts
    integrated, 110

Taxes, 5, 27, 106
Technological changes, 15
Technological price decreases, 119,
    120
Tolerance in costing, 19
Total (or nominal, nominalistic)
    profit, 7, 8, 14, 15, 126
Trading enterprises, 35, 49
Transaction results (see Operating
    results)
Transfer prices, 97

Unrealized profit, 7, 14

Valuation based on net proceeds, 3
Valuation of
    assets, 2, 20
    buildings, 74
    complementary assets, 22, 82
    fixed assets, 21, 71, 133
    foreign assets, 122
    individual assets, 22
    inventories, 21, 60, 133
    land, 21, 71
    machinery, 74
    marketable assets, 122
    non-marketable assets, 123
    obsolete assets, 21, 22, 59
Variable costs, 16
Verification of investments, 25
Volume variances, 14, 31

Work in process, 87

Yield, 4, 6